MW01244003

WHO DO YOU STRUGGLE TO FORGIVE?

21-Day Journal To Explore Forgiveness, Heal Your Heart, And Liberate From Resentment

Blending Our Love, Maryland

Copyright © 2023 by Tuniscia Okeke

All rights reserved. No part of this publication may be reproduced, distributed, or transmitted in any way, form, or by any means, including photocopying, recording, or other electronic or mechanical methods, nor may it be stored in a retrieval system or otherwise be copied for public or private use, other than for "fair use" as brief quotations embodied in articles and reviews without the prior written permission of the author.

Neither the publisher nor author assumes any responsibility for errors, omissions, or contrary interpretations of the subject matter herein. Any perceived slight of any organization or individual is solely unintentional.

Published 2023

Library of Congress Cataloging-in-Publication Data

ISBN: 978-1-962748-18-6 (Print)

ISBN: 978-1-962748-19-3 (eBook)

Printed in the United States of America

WHO DO YOU STRUGGLE TO FORGIVE?

21-Day Journal To Explore Forgiveness, Heal Your Heart, And Liberate From Resentment

TUNISCIA OKEKE

BLENDING OUR LOVE, INC.

DEDICATION

My forgiveness journey began
when I forgave myself first.

Table of Content

Paying It Forward 1

Foreword 5

Introduction : Breaking Free From The Chains Of
Unforgiveness 7

Emotional Disconnections 23

Triggers' Impact On Relationships 27

Release The Struggle 55

Unlocking Healing And Empowerment 59

Day 1: Overcome The Struggle To Forgive Yourself 67

Day 2: Overcome The Struggle To Forgive Your Past
Mistakes 73

Day 3: Overcome The Struggle To Forgive Your
Inner Child..79

Day 4: Overcome The Struggle To Forgive Your Body 85

Day 5: Overcome Your Struggle To Forgive Your
Limiting Thoughts...91

Day 6: Overcome Your Struggle To Forgive Career
Choices 97

Day 7: Overcome The Struggle To Forgive Your
Partner...103

Day 8: Overcome Your Struggle To Forgive Siblings 109

Day 9: Overcome The Struggle To Forgive Your
Children 115

Day 10: Overcome Your Struggle To Forgive Women...... 121

Day 11: Overcome The Struggle To Forgive Your
Current Partner 127

Day 12: Overcome Your Struggle To Forgive
Ex-Partners 133

Day 13: Overcome Your Struggle To Forgive Friends 139

Day 14: Overcome Your Struggle To Forgive God 145

Day 15: Overcome Your Struggle To Forgive Bullies 151

Day 16: Overcome Your Struggles With Money 157

Day 17: Overcome Your Struggle With A Poverty
Mindset 163

Day 18: Overcome Your Struggle With Perfectionism 169

Day 19: Overcome Your Struggle To Forgive Men 175

Day 20: Overcome Struggle To Forgive Racist People 181

Day 21: Overcome Struggle To Forgive People Who
Support Racist People 187

Day 22: I Forgive People For Lying To Me To
"Protect My Feelings" 195

Closing The Chapter Of Unforgiveness 201

Paying It Forward

I'm sharing this message as the author of this 21-day journal on forgiveness, not just with words on these pages but with a story that has shaped my life's purpose. As I embark on this journey with you, I want to share the deeply personal and transformative experiences that led me to write, edit, and self-publish 35 books on forgiveness in less than a year.

My forgiveness journey began when I was 24, a pivotal age when life often feels like an open book, brimming with hope and dreams. Then, my mother called me on a seemingly ordinary Monday morning, and with those words, she unraveled the narrative of my life. She revealed that the man I had believed to be my father for all those years was, in fact, not my biological father.

The weight of that revelation was crushing. It was as if the ground beneath me had shifted, leaving me unsteady and disoriented. But what shook me to my core was not the revelation itself but the sudden rupture of trust in my mother—the person I had always looked up to as a paragon of love, trustworthiness, and honesty.

In the wake of this revelation, I spiraled into a deep pit of resentment, anger, and pain. I grappled with a profound sense of betrayal and felt adrift in a sea of unanswered questions. It was a turbulent period in my life, and for 17 long years, I carried the heavy burden of unforgiveness.

Then, something remarkable happened that would alter the course of my life forever. I noticed a pattern in my relationship with my children. They treated me with a lack of respect and love, leaving me bewildered and hurt. In desperation, I turned to prayer one day, seeking answers from a higher source.

God's voice whispered into my heart in that sacred space of prayer and introspection, revealing a profound truth "I taught them how to love me by the way I loved my mother."

Those words struck me like lightning, piercing through the fog of my confusion. It was an awakening—a profound realization that, in my quest for revenge against my mother, I had unwittingly passed on the energy of resentment to my children. I had normalized my hurtful behaviors as the way we should treat our mothers.

On my 40th birthday, I consciously confronted my soul's deepest and darkest corners. I embarked on a journey of healing, self-forgiveness, and forgiveness of my mother. My primary motivation was to restore my relationship with my children and teach them how to pass on healing, love, and forgiveness to their children.

That six-year odyssey of healing was transformative beyond measure. It led me to write 35 journals, each addressing a facet of forgiveness and healing I encountered on my journey. These journals became my way of reaching out to others grappling with their forgiveness journeys.

Today, I extend a heartfelt invitation to you to embark on this 21-day journey with me. Just as my healing journey began with a single journal, this journal can be your compass for forgiveness, healing, and growth.

I send you loving energy as you navigate through the complexities of your forgiveness journey, and I hope these pages serve as a guiding light toward wholeness and inner peace.

With love and compassion,

Tuniscia O

FOREWORD

A Letter From The Author

Dear Compassionate Readers,

I am immensely grateful for your decision to embark on a soul-nourishing journey through the pages of "Who Do You Struggle To Forgive?" Your presence on this path of forgiveness is a testament to your inner strength and yearning for liberation from resentment.

Over these 21 days, we shall embark on a transformative voyage, exploring the intricate landscapes of forgiveness, understanding, and liberation. This journal is a guiding light, leading you toward deeper self-discovery and the profound freedom forgiveness can offer.

Together, we shall confront the shadows of unforgiveness and embark on a pilgrimage toward light and healing. We will navigate the complexities of past wounds, acknowledging that forgiveness is not about erasing the past but rewriting our future with compassion and grace.

In this journal, you will find space for introspection, room for tears, and moments of cathartic release. As you confront the question, remember it is a journey towards self-liberation and emotional well-being.

With each passing day, you will discover that forgiveness is not a sign of weakness but a reflection of your strength. It is a gift you give to yourself, a gift that has the power to transform your life in unimaginable ways.

May you find solace in the healing you will experience, wisdom, and liberation from the weight of resentment. Carry the lessons with you as you navigate your path forward, and let forgiveness be the compass that guides your way.

Thank you for entrusting me to be a part of your healing journey. Together, we shall explore the depths of forgiveness and find the profound liberation that awaits us.

With heartfelt gratitude and warmest wishes for your transformation,

Tuniscia O

Breaking Free From The Chains Of Unforgiveness

Introduction

In the tapestry of human experience, forgiveness is a thread woven through the intricacies of relationships, experiences, and personal growth. Yet, this seemingly simple act often eludes us, entwining itself with our emotions, memories, and perceptions. This book, titled Who Do You Struggle To Forgive, explores the profound journey toward forgiveness—an expedition that holds the potential to heal wounds, release burdens, and reshape our lives.

We each carry stories of hurt, betrayal, disappointment, and pain. These stories may be etched into the corners of our hearts by those who were supposed to uplift us, by circumstances that left us broken, or by our missteps that continue to haunt us. As we walk through life, these stories can become anchors, tethering us to the past and limiting our ability to embrace the present and future fully.

Forgiveness is not about condoning actions or forgetting the pain. It is about releasing the grip of resentment, anger, and attachment to the pain that holds us captive. Forgiveness is the key that unlocks the door to healing, growth, and transformation. It is a gift we give ourselves—a chance to reclaim our power, find inner peace, and move forward unburdened by the weight of the past.

Who Do You Struggle To Forgive is a roadmap for traversing the landscape of forgiveness—a landscape that can be both treacherous and liberating. Through the pages of this book, we will explore the intricacies of unforgiveness, dissect the barriers that hinder our progress, and uncover the path to forgiveness, healing, and growth.

We will delve into the stories of those who have navigated the tumultuous waters of forgiveness and emerged stronger, wiser, and more empowered. Their journeys are testaments to the human spirit's capacity for resilience and transformation. Their experiences remind us that forgiveness is not a sign of weakness but a testament to our strength and ability to rise above pain.

As we journey together, we will address the struggles that may arise when seeking forgiveness, such as the tussle between justice and mercy, whether to forgive ourselves and the challenges of forgiving those who may never apologize. We will explore how unforgiveness affects our emotional well-being, physical health, relationships, and even our ability to reach our fullest potential.

Through practical insights, transformative exercises, and heartfelt stories, Who Do You Struggle To Forgive offers a toolkit for navigating the path of forgiveness. It empowers readers to step into their own stories, rewrite their narratives, and release the grip of the past. It provides strategies to dismantle the barriers that keep us trapped in resentment and self-imposed limitations, and it guides us toward the profound realization that forgiveness is a gift we give ourselves—one that allows us to be free.

The Big "V"

This journal is an invitation to discover the transformative power of forgiveness and embrace the fullness of life that awaits beyond the chains of unforgiveness. As we embark on this journey together, let us open our hearts, shed the weight of the past, and find the courage to forgive—to heal, grow, and embrace the limitless possibilities.

Vulnerability is the lantern we carry into the dark caverns of our inner world. It grants us the strength to confront our deepest fears, acknowledge lingering resentments, and address unresolved trauma. As we peel back the layers of protection we've built around our hearts, we gain a clearer understanding of the hidden triggers that often control our reactions and behaviors.

This process isn't about wallowing in pain or dwelling on past wounds; it's about facing them head-on with compassion and self-acceptance. Vulnerability empowers us to say, "Yes, these experiences have shaped me, but they don't define me." It offers the opportunity to release the weight of unforgiveness and heal the scars silently festering.

Moreover, vulnerability unveils the subconscious patterns that keep us from reaching our full potential. It enables us to identify self-sabotaging behaviors and thought processes. By shining a light on these hidden obstacles, we can begin dismantling them, allowing personal growth and transformation to flourish.

In the end, vulnerability is not a weakness but a profound strength. It takes great courage to expose our vulnerabilities and confront our inner demons. Through this courageous act, we find liberation, authenticity, and a deeper connection with ourselves and others. The key unlocks the door to self-discovery, personal growth, and the path to becoming our truest and most empowered selves.

Conscious Fears

Conscious fears are the fears we can readily identify in our lives. The anxieties, worries, and concerns often occupy our thoughts and impact our decisions. We are aware of these fears, yet they can be elusive, lurking in our minds and influencing our behavior subtly.

Acknowledging these conscious fears is a vital step in self-discovery and personal growth. When we confront them with vulnerability, we can understand their origins, triggers, and how they have held us back. This self-awareness empowers us to make conscious choices and proactively address these fears.

Moreover, we can develop strategies to overcome our conscious fears by shining a light on them. We can challenge the limiting beliefs that fuel these fears and replace them with empowering and positive thoughts. Through vulnerability, we learn to navigate the terrain of our fears with courage and self-compassion.

In essence, vulnerability opens the door to conscious fears, allowing us to examine them closely and ultimately transcend their grip on our lives. Through this process, we find the freedom to move forward, unencumbered by the fears that once held us captive, and embrace a life filled with authenticity, growth, and empowerment.

Subconscious Fears

Subconscious fears are the hidden, often deeply ingrained anxieties and insecurities that reside beneath the surface of our consciousness. Although not readily apparent, these fears play a significant role in shaping our thoughts, emotions, and behaviors. They stem from past experiences, traumas, and belief systems absorbed into our subconscious mind over time.

Vulnerability is the key that unlocks the door to our subconscious fears. When we allow ourselves to be vulnerable, we create a space for these hidden fears to emerge. This can be a challenging process, as it requires us to confront and explore the layers of our psyche where these fears reside.

We gain a deeper understanding of ourselves and our motivations by bringing subconscious fears to light. We uncover the sources of self-doubt, self-sabotage, and patterns of behavior that have held us back. This awareness empowers us to address these fears, challenge their validity, and work towards healing and transformation.

Ultimately, vulnerability helps us navigate the complex terrain of our subconscious mind, allowing us to release the grip of these hidden fears and reclaim our power. As we integrate this self-awareness into our journey of self-discovery and personal growth, we become better equipped to make conscious choices, break free from self-limiting patterns, and live a life aligned with our true desires and potential.

Resentments And Unforgiveness

Resentment and unforgiveness are emotional burdens that can weigh us down and hinder our personal growth. Often, we carry these feelings deep within ourselves, allowing them to fester and disrupt our emotional well-being. Vulnerability offers us a path to address and release these toxic emotions.

When we embrace vulnerability, we create an opportunity to examine our resentments and unforgiveness. We allow ourselves to acknowledge the hurt, anger, and disappointment that may have accumulated over the years. By doing so, we can begin the process of healing and forgiveness.

Expressing our feelings in a vulnerable and authentic manner is a powerful way to release the grip of resentment. It enables us to communicate our pain and disappointment to the person involved or through self-reflection and journaling. This expression is not about blame but about freeing ourselves from the emotional weight we've been carrying.

Forgiveness, another vital aspect of this process, becomes more accessible through vulnerability. When we acknowledge our pain and the pain of others involved, we can choose to let go of the resentment and grant ourselves the gift of forgiveness. This act of forgiveness is not necessarily about condoning the actions that hurt us but about releasing the emotional bonds that have kept us tethered to the past.

In the end, vulnerability serves as a bridge to emotional liberation. It helps us navigate the complex terrain of resentments and unforgiveness, offering us a pathway to healing and inner peace. Through vulnerability, we can release the burdens of the past and move forward with greater clarity, compassion, and resilience.

Trauma

Trauma can shape our behaviors, beliefs, and emotions, whether from childhood experiences or later in life. Often, these traumatic events remain buried deep within our subconscious, exerting an invisible but powerful influence on our lives. Vulnerability becomes a potent tool in addressing and healing from trauma.

By embracing vulnerability, we create a safe space to explore our traumatic experiences. This exploration involves acknowledging the pain, fear, and distress associated with the trauma. It allows us to express our emotions through therapy, support groups, or introspective journaling.

One of the key benefits of vulnerability in trauma healing is that it fosters a sense of safety and support. Sharing our trauma stories with trusted individuals or professionals can be incredibly therapeutic. It allows us to externalize the pain and, in doing so, take the first steps toward processing and integrating these experiences into our narratives.

Furthermore, vulnerability enables us to seek the help we may need, such as therapy or counseling, to navigate the complexities of trauma. It invites us to reach out and connect with those who can guide us on our healing journey.

In essence, vulnerability empowers us to confront and heal from the traumatic wounds of our past. It's a courageous step toward breaking free from trauma and reclaiming our emotional well-being. We can rewrite our stories through vulnerability, finding resilience and strength in the face of adversity.

Hidden Triggers

Hidden triggers are like landmines in our emotional landscape, ready to explode at unexpected moments. These triggers are often deeply rooted in past experiences and can elicit intense emotional responses that baffle us. Vulnerability serves as a compass, guiding us through uncovering and understanding these hidden triggers.

When we embrace vulnerability, we create a space for introspection and self-exploration. We can delve into moments when we've reacted strongly to seemingly innocuous situations and ask ourselves, "Why did that trigger such a strong response?" This inquiry allows us to trace our emotional reactions back to their source.

Hidden triggers are often linked to past traumas, unmet needs, or unresolved conflicts. Vulnerability allows us to shine a light on these triggers and connect them to specific experiences. This process can be uncomfortable but is essential for personal growth.

Once we identify our hidden triggers, vulnerability empowers us to work through them. We can seek support, such as therapy or self-help resources, to address the underlying issues and develop healthier responses. Over time, vulnerability helps us replace knee-jerk reactions with conscious, intentional choices.

In essence, vulnerability is the key that unlocks the door to understanding and managing hidden triggers.

It enables us to transform moments of emotional turmoil into opportunities for growth and healing, ultimately leading to greater emotional resilience and well-being.

Barriers Holding Us Back

Both visible and invisible barriers can stand between us and our true potential. These barriers often go unnoticed until we open ourselves to vulnerability and self-examination. Vulnerability acts as a spotlight, illuminating the obstacles hindering our progress.

Some barriers may be external, such as societal expectations, discrimination, or limited opportunities. Vulnerability empowers us to acknowledge these external forces and seek ways to overcome or navigate them.

However, many internal barriers are deeply rooted in our beliefs, fears, and self-perceptions. Vulnerability helps us uncover these internal obstacles, such as self-doubt, fear of failure, or imposter syndrome. It allows us to confront these barriers head-on and challenge the narratives that have held us back.

We gain the courage to break down these barriers as we embrace vulnerability. We can seek support through therapy, self-help resources, or mentorship to address these internal challenges. Vulnerability enables us to replace limiting beliefs with empowering ones, allowing us to move forward confidently.

In essence, vulnerability is the catalyst for identifying and dismantling the barriers holding us back. It is the key to unlocking our true potential and charting a path toward personal growth, fulfillment, and authenticity.

Secret Struggles

Secret struggles often weigh heavily on our hearts, hidden from the world as we grapple with them in solitude. These hidden battles can be sources of immense stress, anxiety, and inner turmoil. They may range from personal insecurities and past traumas to unexpressed emotions and unmet needs.

Vulnerability becomes the bridge to inner peace in these secret struggles. When we muster the courage to share our burdens, even with one trusted person, we unburden ourselves emotionally. Opening up and being honest about our struggles allows us to release pent-up emotions and start the healing process.

Through vulnerability, we find understanding and empathy from others. They may have experienced similar struggles or can offer support and guidance. This connection with others alleviates the isolation often accompanying secret struggles and reminds us that we are not alone.

Furthermore, the vulnerability enables us to confront and process our inner turmoil directly. By expressing our emotions and experiences, we gain clarity and perspective. We can seek professional help or engage in self-reflection to address the root causes of our struggles and work towards resolutions.

Ultimately, vulnerability offers a pathway to inner peace by dismantling the walls of isolation and self-silencing. It empowers us to seek support, express our truths, and embark on healing and self-acceptance. In embracing vulnerability, we pave the way for inner peace to flourish.

In essence, vulnerability is the compass that guides us through the uncharted territory of our emotions and psyche. It's the tool we use to dig deep, unearth our innermost struggles, and pave the way for profound healing and transformation. Embracing vulnerability isn't a sign of weakness; it's an act of immense courage that leads to self-discovery and empowerment.

Emotional Disconnections

E motional disconnection can be a significant hurdle when forgiving people or situations. Our ability to forgive is deeply intertwined with our emotional state, and when we're emotionally disconnected, forgiveness becomes a more challenging process. Let's explore how emotional disconnection can hinder forgiveness and ways to bridge this gap.

Lack Of Empathy

Emotional disconnection often means that we struggle to empathize with others. When forgiving, it's crucial to understand the perspectives and emotions of the person who hurt us. Emotional disconnection can make it difficult to put ourselves in their shoes, making it harder to find empathy and, consequently, to forgive.

Suppressed Emotions

Emotional disconnection often goes hand in hand with suppressing emotions. Forgiveness can be stunted when we don't allow ourselves to feel and express our feelings. Forgiveness often requires acknowledging our pain, anger, and resentment; if these emotions are buried deep within us, forgiveness becomes elusive.

Difficulty In Letting Go

Emotional disconnection can make it hard to let go of the hurt and resentment we hold onto. Forgiveness involves releasing these negative emotions and consciously deciding to move forward. When we're emotionally disconnected, we may find it challenging to release these feelings, keeping us in a cycle of unforgiveness.

Inability To Communicate

Communication is often a crucial component of forgiveness. We need to express our feelings and thoughts, which requires emotional connection. When emotionally disconnected, we may struggle to articulate our pain or engage in meaningful conversations with those we must forgive.

So, how can we bridge this emotional gap and work towards forgiveness?

Self-Awareness

The first step is recognizing our emotional disconnection. Self-awareness allows us to acknowledge our emotional state and understand how it's impacting our ability to forgive. Journaling or therapy can be helpful tools for gaining this awareness.

Practice Mindfulness

Mindfulness techniques can help us reconnect with our emotions. By being present in the moment and non-judgmentally observing our feelings, we can begin to access and process them.

Seek Support

Sometimes, we can't overcome emotional disconnection on our own. Seeking support from friends, family, or a therapist can provide the emotional connection and understanding needed to work through forgiveness.

Empathy Building

Practice empathy exercises to develop your ability to understand and relate to others' feelings. This can involve reading books or articles from different perspectives, engaging in empathetic conversations, or volunteering to help others.

Emotional Expression

Find healthy ways to express your emotions. This might include talking to a trusted friend or therapist, writing in a journal, or engaging in creative outlets like art or music. Allowing your emotions to surface is a crucial step in the forgiveness process.

Mindful Forgiveness

When you feel emotionally ready, approach forgiveness mindfully. This means acknowledging the hurt, recognizing the humanity in the person who hurt you, and consciously letting go of resentment.

Give It Time

Forgiveness is only sometimes immediate. It's a process that can take time, especially when dealing with deep emotional disconnection. Be patient with yourself and allow the healing process to unfold naturally.

In conclusion, emotional disconnection can indeed make forgiving people or situations more challenging. However, with self-awareness, mindfulness, support, and practice, it is possible to reconnect with your emotions and work towards forgiveness. Remember that forgiveness is a gift you give yourself, allowing you to release resentment and find peace within.

Triggers' Impact On Relationships

Triggers can create tension and conflict within relationships. When something or someone activates a trigger, it can lead to emotional outbursts, misunderstandings, or even withdrawal from the relationship. These reactions can strain connections with loved ones, making maintaining healthy and fulfilling relationships difficult.

Triggers have a profound impact on our relationships. When triggered, we often react from a place of heightened emotion, leading to misunderstandings, conflicts, and strained connections with others. Here's how triggers affect our relationships:

Communication Breakdown

Triggers can hinder effective communication. When triggered, we may struggle to express ourselves calmly and rationally. This communication breakdown can lead to arguments and misunderstandings.

Emotional Distance

Triggers can create emotional distance between us and our loved ones. When we react intensely to a trigger, we might withdraw emotionally, leaving our partners or friends feeling shut out and disconnected.

Repetitive Patterns

Triggers often lead to repetitive relationship patterns. If certain topics or behaviors trigger us, we may find ourselves stuck in a cycle of recurring conflicts, making it challenging to move forward and build healthier dynamics.

Conflict Escalation

Triggers can escalate conflicts. What might start as a small disagreement can quickly intensify when triggered emotions come into play, leading to more significant and hurtful arguments.

Underlying Resentment

Frequent triggering can foster underlying resentment in relationships. If we don't address our triggers and the emotions they bring up, resentment can build over time, eroding the foundation of trust and intimacy.

Impact On Intimacy

Triggers can affect intimacy in various ways. Emotional withdrawal and unresolved conflicts can hinder emotional and physical intimacy, causing strain in romantic relationships.

Stress On Support Systems

When triggers impact our relationships, it can also affect our support systems. Friends and family may become caught in the crossfire or feel burdened by the ongoing conflicts, potentially straining these important relationships.

Addressing triggers within relationships requires self-awareness, open communication, and a commitment to personal growth. It's essential to recognize when you've been triggered and take steps to manage your emotional responses. Seeking support from a therapist or counselor can be valuable in learning how to navigate triggers and improve relationship dynamics. Understanding and addressing triggers can lead to healthier, more fulfilling relationships built on trust, empathy, and effective communication.

How Triggers Impact Forgiveness

Triggers are emotional reactions or responses to certain people, relationships, or situations that can cause significant life struggles. These triggers often stem from past experiences, trauma, or unresolved issues and can impact our ability to navigate life's challenges effectively. Let's delve into how triggers can affect our interactions and relationships and explore strategies for managing them.

Triggers, those emotional landmines that can explode unexpectedly, often create significant hurdles in our journey toward forgiveness. These triggers are deeply rooted in past experiences and traumas and can stir up intense emotions that make forgiveness seem almost impossible. Let's explore the intricate relationship between triggers and our struggles when forgiving people, relationships, and situations.

Repetition Of Patterns

Triggers often leads us to repeat patterns of behavior or responses shaped by past experiences. For example, if you have a trigger related to feeling abandoned, you may push people away to protect yourself, even if they have no intention of leaving.

Triggers are like emotional landmines that can send us spiraling into behavior patterns rooted in our past experiences. These patterns often manifest in response to our perceived threats, even if those threats aren't real or immediate. Here's how triggers can lead to the repetition of behavioral patterns:

Protective Mechanism

Triggers activate our brain's fight-or-flight response, causing us to react as if we're in danger. For example, if you have a trigger related to feeling abandoned, your brain might interpret certain situations as a threat to your emotional safety. To protect yourself, you might push people away, even when they have no intention of leaving. This is a protective mechanism rooted in past experiences of abandonment.

Emotional Memory

Triggers are often tied to emotional memories from our past. When activated, a trigger can bring back intense emotions and sensations associated with those memories. These emotions can overwhelm our rational thinking and cause us to act in ways that mirror past responses to similar situations.

Reinforced Neural Pathways

Over time, our responses to triggers become ingrained in our neural pathways. The more we react a certain way to a trigger, the stronger those neural pathways become. This makes breaking free from these patterns increasingly difficult, even when we recognize their negative impact.

Self-Fulfilling Prophecy

Triggers can create a self-fulfilling prophecy. For instance, if your trigger leads you to push people away to avoid feeling abandoned, your actions may lead to the very outcome you fear, reinforcing your belief that abandonment is inevitable.

Breaking free from these patterns requires self-awareness, self-compassion, and a willingness to challenge our automatic responses. Therapy and personal growth work can be instrumental in identifying triggers, understanding their roots, and developing healthier ways to respond. By recognizing and addressing these patterns, we can regain control over our behavior and forge more positive and fulfilling relationships.

Heightened Emotional Reactivity

Triggers can send our emotions into overdrive. We might react with intense anger or sadness, making it difficult to approach forgiveness from a place of calm and rationality.

Heightened emotional reactivity is a common response to triggers. When we encounter situations or stimuli that activate our triggers, our emotions can escalate rapidly and intensify. This heightened emotional state often manifests as intense anger, sadness, anxiety, or a combination of these emotions. Here's how heightened emotional reactivity can impact our ability to approach forgiveness:

Loss Of Rationality

When our emotions are heightened, our ability to think rationally and make clear, reasoned decisions can be compromised. We may react impulsively, driven by our emotional intensity rather than thoughtful consideration.

Ineffective Communication

Heightened emotional reactivity can lead to communication breakdowns. We may struggle to express ourselves clearly, resorting to emotional outbursts or withdrawal, which hinders productive conversations and conflict resolution.

Prolonged Negative Feelings

Intense emotional reactions can prolong negative feelings and resentments. Instead of moving toward forgiveness, we may become entrenched in our emotional responses, making it challenging to let go and find closure.

Physical Stress

Heightened emotions can also take a toll on our physical well-being. Increased stress hormones and physiological responses to intense emotions can lead to headaches, sleep disturbances, and other health issues, further complicating our ability to engage in forgiveness.

To address heightened emotional reactivity in the context of forgiveness, it's essential to practice emotional regulation techniques. These may include deep breathing exercises, mindfulness practices, and self-soothing strategies. Seeking support from a therapist or counselor can also be invaluable in developing emotional resilience and learning to manage intense emotional reactions.

By gaining control over our emotional responses, we can approach forgiveness with greater clarity and a calmer state of mind, allowing us to engage in productive conversations, release negative emotions, and, ultimately, achieve emotional healing and closure.

Disrupted Emotional Healing

Disrupted emotional healing is a significant challenge triggered by past traumas or unresolved emotional wounds. When we are on a path of emotional healing, we often work diligently to process and overcome these wounds. However, triggers can disrupt this process and send us back into a cycle of negative emotions and unhealed pain.

Here's how triggers can disrupt emotional healing:

Reopened Wounds

Triggers can reopen emotional wounds that we thought were healing or had already healed. These wounds may resurface with the same intensity as when they were first experienced, causing emotional distress and re-traumatization.

Stagnation

Progress made in emotional healing can come to a standstill when triggers are encountered. Instead of moving forward, we may find ourselves stuck in a loop of reliving past traumas, which can hinder personal growth and recovery.

Emotional Overwhelm

Triggers often lead to overwhelming emotional reactions. These intense emotions can be difficult to manage, making it challenging to focus on healing and self-care.

Self-Doubt

Encountering triggers may lead to self-doubt as we question our ability to heal and move beyond our past pain. This self-doubt can erode our self-esteem and confidence.

To address disrupted emotional healing caused by triggers, it's essential to implement self-care practices, seek support from therapists or support groups, and engage in trauma-informed therapies like EMDR or cognitive-behavioral therapy. These approaches can help us navigate triggers more effectively and resume our journey toward emotional healing.

While triggers can be powerful disruptors, they can also be opportunities for deeper understanding and growth. By addressing triggers head-on and incorporating them into our healing process, we can gradually build resilience and work through the lingering effects of past traumas, ultimately achieving emotional wholeness and well-being.

Stress And Emotional Overwhelm

Stress and emotional overwhelm are common responses to triggers, and they can significantly impact our well-being. Triggers often stem from past traumas or painful experiences, which can stir up intense emotions and disrupt our emotional equilibrium.

When we encounter triggers, our body's stress response can be activated. This triggers the release of stress hormones like cortisol and adrenaline, preparing us for a "fight or flight" response. However, in situations related to emotional triggers, neither fighting nor fleeing is typically appropriate or productive. Instead, we may find ourselves in a state of emotional overwhelm, struggling to manage our reactions.

This emotional overwhelm can manifest in various ways:

Anxiety

Triggers can lead to heightened anxiety, characterized by racing thoughts, restlessness, and impending doom. We may constantly worry about encountering similar triggers or re-traumatization.

Anger

Some triggers evoke intense anger and irritability, causing us to react defensively or lash out at others.

Sadness

For others, triggers can bring forth deep sadness and despair, leading to depression-like symptoms and withdrawal from daily activities.

Physical Symptoms

Stress and emotional overwhelm can manifest in physical symptoms such as headaches, digestive issues, and sleep disturbances.

To address stress and emotional overwhelm triggered by past traumas or painful experiences, it's essential to develop healthy coping mechanisms. This may include mindfulness practices, relaxation techniques, and seeking support from therapists or support groups. We can gradually regain emotional balance and resilience by acknowledging and working through these emotions.

Revisiting Emotional Wounds

Revisiting emotional wounds through triggers can be a profoundly unsettling experience. Triggers can transport us back in time, mentally and emotionally, to the very moments when we first experienced pain, trauma, or distress. When confronted with a trigger, it's as if we are reliving those past events, complete with the same intense emotions and vulnerabilities we felt then.

This phenomenon can make forgiveness and healing even more challenging. Here's why:

Intense Emotional Resurgence

Triggers bring back the same intense emotions we felt during the original hurtful or traumatic experience. This resurgence of emotions can be overwhelming and make it difficult to approach forgiveness from a calm and rational perspective.

Lack of Emotional Distance

To forgive it often helps to gain some emotional distance from the past event. Triggers, however, blur this distance, making it hard to view the situation objectively and make peace with it.

Reinforced Negative Beliefs

Triggers can reinforce negative beliefs or self-perceptions formed during the initial emotional wound. For example, if you felt unworthy or unlovable during a past hurt, a trigger can bring these feelings back to the surface, making forgiveness seem even more distant.

To navigate this challenging aspect of triggers, practicing self-compassion and patience is important. Recognize that when triggers resurface old wounds, it's a sign that more healing must be done. Seek support from therapists or support groups to process these emotions and work towards forgiveness. By addressing the underlying emotional wounds and gaining a deeper understanding of their impact on your present, you can move closer to forgiveness and healing.

Difficulty In Problem Solving

Difficulty in problem-solving often arises when triggers are activated. These emotional reactions can cloud our judgment and hinder our ability to approach challenges with clarity and rationality. Here's how triggers can impact problem-solving:

Emotional Reactivity

When a trigger is activated, our emotions can run high. This heightened emotional state can make approaching problems with a calm and level-headed mindset challenging. Instead, we may react impulsively, driven by intense feelings, which can lead to rash decisions.

Narrowed Perspective

Triggers often focus our attention on the source of our emotional distress, making it difficult to see the bigger picture. This narrowed perspective can limit our ability to consider alternative solutions or perspectives when facing challenges.

Conflict Escalation

In interpersonal situations, triggers can escalate conflicts rather than resolve them. When triggered, we may become defensive, argumentative, or withdraw from the situation altogether, preventing productive problem-solving and communication.

Delayed Resolutions

Triggers can prolong the time it takes to find solutions. The emotional turmoil triggered by past wounds can distract us from addressing the present issue, leading to delays in resolving problems.

To overcome these challenges, it's essential to recognize when triggers are at play and take steps to manage them effectively. This may involve practicing mindfulness to stay present in the moment, using relaxation techniques to regulate emotions, seeking support from a therapist or counselor to process triggering events, and working on developing emotional intelligence to navigate challenges with greater clarity and empathy. By addressing triggers and their impact on problem-solving, we can improve our ability to face challenges constructively and find solutions that align with our goals and values.

Resistance To Vulnerability

Resistance to vulnerability is a common response when triggers are activated in the forgiveness process. Triggers remind us of past hurts and traumas, making us defensive and resistant to emotional opening up. Here's how resistance to vulnerability can impact forgiveness:

Defensiveness

When triggered, we may instinctively use emotional walls as a protective mechanism. These walls shield us from further emotional pain but also block the path to vulnerability and the emotional connection necessary for forgiveness.

Avoidance

Resisting vulnerability can lead to avoidance behaviors. We may avoid confronting the person or situation that triggered us, thinking it's safer to keep our distance. However, this avoidance can hinder the forgiveness process, as it doesn't allow for the necessary communication and understanding.

Emotional Shutdown

Triggers can sometimes lead to an emotional shutdown, where we numb ourselves to feelings as a way to cope. In this state, we may be unable to access the emotions required for forgiveness, such as empathy and compassion.

Lack Of Trust

Resistance to vulnerability often stems from a lack of trust, especially if past experiences have taught us that opening up leads to more pain. This lack of trust can make it challenging to extend forgiveness.

To address resistance to vulnerability in the forgiveness process, it's essential to recognize when it's happening and take deliberate steps to overcome it:

Self-Reflection

Take time to reflect on why you're resistant to vulnerability. What past experiences or beliefs are contributing to this resistance? Understanding the root causes can be the first step toward overcoming it.

Mindfulness

Practice mindfulness techniques to stay present in the forgiveness process. Mindfulness can help you acknowledge your resistance without judgment and gradually open up to vulnerability.

Seek Support

Engage in conversations with trusted friends, family members, or a therapist who can provide a safe space for vulnerability. Sharing your feelings and experiences with someone you trust can help you build confidence in vulnerability.

Empathy

Try to empathize with the person you're forgiving. Understand that vulnerability is a two-way street, and opening up emotionally creates an opportunity for understanding and healing on both sides.

By addressing resistance to vulnerability, you can create a more conducive environment for forgiveness, fostering deeper emotional connections and ultimately finding peace and closure.

Struggles In Communication

Struggles in communication often accompany triggers, making it challenging to navigate the forgiveness process effectively. Here's how triggers can impact communication and forgiveness:

Defensiveness

When triggered, we may become defensive, ready to protect ourselves from further harm. This defensiveness can manifest as interrupting, arguing, or shutting down during conversations, preventing productive communication.

Ineffective Expression

Triggers can cloud our ability to express our feelings and needs clearly. We might struggle to articulate our pain, anger, or desires, making it challenging for the other party to understand and empathize.

Misinterpretation

On the flip side, when we're triggered, we may misinterpret the words or actions of others. Our emotional state can lead us to attribute negative intentions to benign statements or actions, causing unnecessary conflicts.

Avoidance

Triggers can also lead to avoidance of important conversations. We might steer clear of discussing the issue that triggered us, thinking it's easier to avoid the discomfort. However, avoiding communication can hinder the forgiveness process.

Lack Of Empathy

Empathetic listening is crucial for forgiveness, but triggers can diminish our capacity for empathy. When we're in emotional turmoil, it becomes challenging to truly understand the perspective and feelings of the person we're forgiving.

To address communication struggles in forgiveness:

Pause And Reflect

When triggered, take a moment to pause and reflect on your emotional state. Ask yourself if this is the right time for a conversation or if you need time to calm down and collect your thoughts.

Active Listening

Practice active listening by truly focusing on what the other person is saying rather than formulating your response. Seek to understand their perspective before expressing your own.

"I"-Statements

Use "I" statements to express your feelings and needs without blaming or accusing. For example, say, "I felt hurt when..." instead of "You hurt me when..."

Empathetic Questions

Ask open-ended questions that encourage the other person to share their feelings and perspective. This can foster empathy and understanding on both sides.

Seek Mediation

If communication is consistently challenging, consider involving a neutral third party, such as a therapist or mediator, to facilitate the conversation.

Addressing communication struggles associated with triggers can create a more conducive environment for effective forgiveness conversations, leading to greater understanding and healing.

Fear Of Repeating The Past

The fear of history repeating itself is a common emotional response when dealing with triggers in the forgiveness process. This fear can be a significant obstacle to letting go of anger and resentment. Here's how it impacts the forgiveness journey:

Self-Protective Instinct

When we've been hurt in the past, our instinct is to protect ourselves from future harm. Triggers can activate this self-protective instinct, leading us to believe that forgiving means exposing ourselves to the risk of being hurt again.

Emotional Guardedness

The fear of repeating the past can make us emotionally guarded. We may hesitate to open up or trust others, even if they've shown genuine remorse or changed behavior.

Maintaining Control

Some people hold onto anger and resentment as a way to maintain a sense of control over their lives. They believe that by staying angry, they are preventing a recurrence of the painful experience.

Stagnation In Healing

This fear can stall the healing process. By refusing to forgive, we may remain stuck in the past, unable to move forward and experience emotional growth.

To address the fear of history repeating itself in the forgiveness journey:

Acknowledge The Fear

Recognize that this fear is a natural response to past pain. It's okay to acknowledge and validate your feelings.

Assess The Situation

Consider whether the circumstances that led to the initial hurt are the same as they are now. Has the person or situation changed? Assess if there is a genuine risk of history repeating itself.

Seek Professional Help

If the fear is overwhelming and preventing you from forgiving, consider consulting a therapist or counselor. They can provide guidance and tools to address this fear and facilitate forgiveness.

Focus On Self-Empowerment

Remember that forgiveness is not about surrendering control but about empowering yourself to let go of the emotional burden. It's a choice that you make for your well-being.

Set Boundaries

If necessary, establish healthy boundaries to protect yourself while allowing forgiveness. Boundaries can provide a sense of safety.

By addressing the fear of history repeating itself and finding a balance between forgiveness and self-protection, you can embark on a healing journey that allows you to release the weight of the past and move forward with greater emotional freedom.

Intrusive Thoughts

Intrusive thoughts are unwelcome and distressing mental patterns that unresolved issues and past traumas can trigger. When it comes to forgiveness, triggers can indeed lead to intrusive thoughts about the past and the "what ifs" and "could haves." Here's how these thoughts can impact the forgiveness process:

Rumination

Triggers can set off a cycle of rumination where we continuously replay past events and scenarios in our minds. This constant mental replay can be emotionally draining and prevent us from moving forward.

Self-Blame

Intrusive thoughts often involve self-blame and self-criticism. We may fixate on what we could have done differently, leading to feelings of guilt and regret.

Obsessive Focus

Triggers can cause us to focus on the details of the hurtful event obsessively. This hyper-focus can magnify the pain and make forgiveness seem even more challenging.

Stalled Healing

Intrusive thoughts can stall the healing process by keeping us tethered to the past. They prevent us from fully embracing the present and future as we remain preoccupied with what has already occurred.

To manage intrusive thoughts and support the forgiveness journey:

Mindfulness

Practice mindfulness techniques to become more aware of intrusive thoughts when they arise. Mindfulness helps you observe these thoughts without judgment and gradually let them go.

Self-Compassion

Cultivate self-compassion by recognizing that everyone makes mistakes, including yourself. Understand that you did the best you could at the time, given your circumstances.

Grounding Techniques

When intrusive thoughts become overwhelming, use grounding techniques to bring yourself back to the present moment. This can include deep breathing, focusing on your senses, or engaging in physical activities.

Professional Help

If intrusive thoughts persist and significantly impact your daily life, consider seeking help from a therapist or counselor. They can provide specialized strategies for managing intrusive thoughts and supporting forgiveness.

Forgiveness Practice

Incorporate forgiveness practices that focus on letting go of the past and embracing the present. Visualization exercises and forgiveness journaling can be helpful in this regard.

Forgiveness is a process, and managing intrusive thoughts is part of that journey. By addressing these thoughts with patience and self-compassion, you can gradually release their grip on your emotional well-being and work towards forgiveness and healing.

Release The Struggle

Self-Awareness

Self-awareness is indeed the foundational step in addressing triggers and working towards forgiveness. By acknowledging and understanding the triggers that evoke strong emotional reactions, individuals can gain insights into their past experiences, fears, and unresolved issues that contribute to these reactions. This self-awareness forms the basis for developing strategies to manage triggers, cultivate empathy, and ultimately embark on the path of forgiveness. It empowers individuals to take control of their emotional responses and make conscious choices in their forgiveness journey, leading to healing and personal growth.

Emotional Regulation

Emotional regulation is a vital skill in handling triggers and fostering forgiveness. Managing one's emotional reactions when triggered can prevent impulsive responses driven by anger or hurt. Techniques such as deep breathing, mindfulness, or pausing to regain composure enable individuals to respond from a place of emotional balance and rationality. By regulating emotions, individuals can engage in more constructive and empathetic conversations, fostering understanding and ultimately facilitating forgiveness.

Seek Support

Seeking support is a crucial step in managing triggers and working towards forgiveness. A therapist, counselor, or coach can help you delve into the underlying causes of your triggers, offering insights and coping strategies. Trusted friends and family can provide emotional support and a safe space to discuss feelings. With support, you can better understand your triggers, develop healthier responses, and navigate the path to forgiveness more effectively.

Communication Skills

Improving your communication skills is essential in managing triggers and fostering forgiveness. Active listening and assertiveness can help you express your feelings and needs effectively. By communicating openly and empathetically, you can reduce the negative impact of triggers on your relationships, allowing for more meaningful and constructive conversations.

Healing Past Trauma

Healing past trauma is crucial if your triggers are deeply rooted in those experiences. Seeking therapy or trauma-specific treatments can provide you with the tools and support needed to address and heal these wounds. By addressing the source of your triggers, you can gradually reduce their impact and work towards forgiveness and emotional well-being.

Mindfulness

Practicing mindfulness is a valuable tool to stay present and grounded when triggers arise. Mindfulness techniques enable you to observe your reactions without judgment, allowing you to create space for healthier responses to your triggers. This awareness and presence at the moment can be instrumental in managing and ultimately overcoming the challenges posed by triggers, fostering forgiveness and emotional healing.

Set Boundaries

Setting clear and healthy boundaries is crucial in managing triggers. These boundaries serve as a protective shield, preventing you from being repeatedly exposed to situations or people that consistently trigger negative reactions. By defining and communicating your limits assertively, you create a space where you have greater control over your emotional responses. This empowerment can be a significant step towards healing and forgiveness, as it allows you to choose how and when you engage with triggering situations, ultimately leading to greater emotional well-being.

Forgiveness Education

Forgiveness education is a powerful tool in navigating triggers and working towards forgiveness. By educating yourself about the nature of forgiveness and its numerous benefits, you gain valuable insights into how forgiveness can positively impact your overall well-being. Understanding that forgiveness is a gift you give yourself, rather than condoning the actions of others, can be a motivating factor in your journey to work through triggers and release the burden of resentment. This knowledge empowers you to make informed choices about forgiveness and offers a path toward healing and emotional freedom.

Slow And Steady

Taking a slow and steady approach to forgiveness is essential, especially when dealing with triggers. It's crucial to be patient with yourself during this process. Forgiveness is not a quick fix; it's a journey that often requires time and self-compassion. When triggers are involved, emotions can be intense, and healing may take longer. Allow yourself the space and understanding to navigate forgiveness at your own pace. Rushing the process can lead to added stress and hinder your ability to achieve genuine forgiveness. Embrace the journey, and trust that you will find the healing and peace you seek with time.

Triggers can indeed cause struggles in our interactions, relationships, and situations, but with self-awareness, emotional regulation, and support, managing and minimizing their impact is possible. You can work towards healthier relationships and a more fulfilling life by addressing these triggers.

Unlocking Healing And Empowerment

In the corridors of our minds, memories, and emotions are entwined, creating a tapestry of experiences that shape our perspectives and influence our choices. Within this intricate web lie moments of joy and the burdens of pain, triumph, and the shackles of regret. Journaling, a powerful tool at our disposal, offers a pathway to navigate these corridors, releasing the struggles of the past, quieting the mental torment, and scripting a future imbued with empowerment and growth.

The Liberating Act Of Expression

Imagine your journal as a trusted confidant—a silent listener who welcomes every thought, emotion, and reflection without judgment. When we pen to paper, we externalize the chaos within us, inviting our thoughts and feelings to materialize outside ourselves. In this act of expression, we free our minds from the burden of carrying the weight alone.

Through journaling, we create space to voice our struggles, grievances, and sorrows. We unburden our hearts and minds, allowing our stories to breathe. By acknowledging these emotions, we begin to loosen their grip on us, creating room for healing to take root.

Rewriting Our Narratives

As we pour ourselves onto the pages, we initiate a transformative process—our stories are no longer confined within us; they find a new home on paper. This act of externalization is akin to rewriting the chapters of our lives. We hold the pen not only to recount our past but also to shape our future.

Journaling invites us to scrutinize the narratives we have internalized. Are these narratives fostering growth or holding us hostage to past pain? By engaging in introspection, we can edit our stories, question limiting beliefs, and craft a narrative that resonates with our aspirations.

Empowerment Through Reflection

In the quiet solitude of journaling, we unearth gems of insight that often remain hidden amidst the din of daily life. As we flip through the pages, thought, emotion, and behavior patterns emerge. These patterns are breadcrumbs leading us to self-awareness, an essential foundation for change.

With each reflection, we gain clarity about our struggles and their roots. We uncover the triggers that ignite our mental torment and the sources of our strength. Armed with this knowledge, we become architects of transformation. We are no longer victims of circumstance but empowered agents of change.

Mapping The Journey Forward

Journaling becomes a roadmap—a guide to charting our way forward. As we lay bare our struggles, we also lay the groundwork for healing. We identify the milestones of progress, the stepping stones toward liberation. Our journal serves as a compass, reminding us of the direction we wish to head.

In each entry, we document not only the struggles but also the triumphs. These moments of victory—no matter how small—remind us of our resilience and capacity to overcome. As we witness our growth and celebrate our wins, our journal becomes a testament to our journey—a story of empowerment and renewal.

The Daily Ritual Of Transformation

Incorporating journaling into our daily routine is a ritual of self-care and self-discovery. It becomes a sacred space where we release the past, tame the mind's turmoil, and step into a promising future. As we embark on this journey, let's embrace the power of daily journaling—a journey that fosters healing, empowers us to reclaim our narratives, and propels us toward a future where the weight of the past no longer defines our trajectory.

With pen in hand and heart open, let our journal pages become a canvas for transformation. Let our stories of struggle evolve into stories of resilience. Let our daily reflections propel us forward, cultivating empowerment as we rewrite our narratives one word at a time.

Harnessing the Power Of Daily Journaling In A Busy Life

In the whirlwind of our modern lives, carving out time for self-care can feel like a monumental challenge. Amidst the demands of work, family, and responsibilities, incorporating daily journaling might seem daunting. However, by embracing a few strategic steps, you can make journaling an integral part of your routine, fostering self-care and personal growth, even amidst a bustling schedule.

Set A Clear Intention

Begin by clarifying why journaling is important to you. Whether it's to release stress, gain insights, or document your journey, a clear intention will keep you motivated and focused.

Start Small

Recognize that even a few minutes of journaling daily can yield significant benefits. Begin with a manageable timeframe, like 5-10 minutes, and gradually increase it as you become more comfortable.

Choose A Consistent Time

Establish a specific time of day for journaling that works best for your schedule. Consistency is critical to making journaling a habit, whether it's in the morning, during lunch breaks, or before bed.

Create A Ritual

Pair your journaling practice with an existing routine. For example, you could journal right after your morning coffee or before winding down for the night. This helps anchor the pattern in your daily life.

Designate A Space

Identify a comfortable and quiet space where you can focus on your journaling. This could be a cozy corner, a park bench, or a peaceful spot in your home.

Embrace Stream Of Consciousness

Don't overthink it. Let your thoughts flow freely onto the pages without judgment. This stream-of-consciousness style can be incredibly cathartic and insightful.

Focus On Quality, Not Quantity

Remember, it's not about how much you write but the depth of your reflections. Even a few sentences can hold significant meaning.

Set Reminders

In the beginning, setting reminders on your phone or using sticky notes can help you remember to journal until it becomes a natural part of your routine.

Celebrate Wins

Acknowledge your achievements in maintaining a journaling practice. Reward yourself for consistency and celebrate the insights and growth that arise.

Embrace Flexibility

Life is dynamic, and some days may be busier than others. Journal for a few minutes on particularly hectic days or jot down a single thought.

Reflect On Progress

Periodically review your journal entries to observe your journey, growth, and patterns. This reflection can be gratifying and motivating.

Adjust As Needed

If your initial approach isn't working, feel free to adapt. The goal is to make journaling a sustainable practice that enhances your well-being.

Practice Self-Compassion

If you miss a day or two, don't be discouraged. Approach journaling with kindness and acknowledge that each day is a fresh opportunity to recommit.

By integrating these steps into your routine, you can harness the power of daily journaling to cultivate self-care and personal growth. Remember, the journaling journey is uniquely yours—celebrate the moments of insight, resilience, and empowerment that unfold as you navigate life's busy currents.

Overcome The Struggle
To Forgive Yourself

Forgiveness Reflection of the Day

Dear Me,

I want you to know that you deserve forgiveness and boundless self-love. As you read these words, remember that your journey is a tapestry woven with triumphs and mistakes, all of which have shaped the incredible person you are today.

Let go of the weight you've been carrying, the burden of past choices and perceived shortcomings. It's time to release the grip of regret and embrace the power of self-forgiveness. Your imperfections are the brushstrokes that make your canvas unique and beautiful. Just as you extend compassion to others, open it to yourself.

Your mistakes do not define you. Instead, you are defined by your resilience, your ability to learn, and your unwavering strength. Every step has led you to this point of growth, wisdom, and self-awareness. Embrace your journey wholeheartedly.

Let self-love be the cornerstone of your existence. Nurture yourself with kindness, understanding, and patience. Speak to yourself as you would to a dear friend—with encouragement and empathy. Celebrate your victories, no matter how small, and acknowledge your efforts in the face of challenges.

Remember, forgiveness and self-love are not one-time achievements but ongoing practices. Whenever self-doubt creeps in, gently remind yourself that you are enough, just as you are. Replace self-criticism with affirmations that nourish your spirit and remind you of your worth.

Allow vulnerability to be your strength. Share your struggles and triumphs openly, knowing your authenticity can inspire and uplift others. You are a guiding light for those who seek the path of self-acceptance.

As you move forward, may your heart be a sanctuary of self-love, forgiveness, and unshakeable belief in your potential. Your journey is a testament to your growth, resilience, and the power of embracing every facet of your being.

With unwavering support and love,

[Your Name]

Meditative Thought of the Day

A symphony of healing arises as I journey through the depths of self-forgiveness. Shadows disperse, revealing an inner light that radiates authenticity. Each step unfurls newfound freedom, a tapestry woven with compassion. The past's grip loosens, making space for growth and renewal.

With forgiveness as my compass, I navigate towards serenity, a realm of self-acceptance and grace. In this transformed landscape, joy is my companion, and the burden of self-blame fades. I savor the present moment, unburdened by yesterday's regrets. As I rise from the ashes of guilt, I emerge stronger, kinder, and whole.

The tapestry of my being is rewoven with threads of resilience and love, a masterpiece of a heart reborn.

Deeper Connection Within

1. What underlying emotions make forgiveness difficult for you, and how have they manifested in your life and relationships?

_____

_____

_____

_____

_____

2. Can you recall a specific incident that has impacted your ability to forgive yourself and others? How has it shaped your perspective?

_____

_____

_____

_____

_____

3. How does forgiving someone or yourself relate to your healing journey and personal growth?

_____

_____

_____

_____

_____

Loving Statements About Me

I release the weight of past mistakes and embrace the power of self-forgiveness.

Forgiveness is my gift to myself, freeing me from resentment.

I forgive myself and others, understanding that growth comes from lessons learned.

Gratitude Reflection of the Day

Today, I am grateful for the journey of self-forgiveness. It's a path toward inner peace and healing that I'm learning to embrace.

Inner Reflections

Overcome The Struggle To Forgive Your Past Mistakes

Forgiveness Reflection of the Day

Dear Me,

I want you to pause for a moment and take a deep breath. As you read these words, remember that you are human—capable of incredible feats and mistakes. Let go of the heavy burden you've carried, the weight of past errors. It's time to release the grip of self-blame and embrace the gentle embrace of grace and self-compassion.

Life is a learning journey, and mistakes are the stepping stones that lead to growth and wisdom. The scars you bear tell stories of resilience and transformation, not failures. You deserve forgiveness, especially from yourself.

Embrace the truth that self-compassion is not a weakness; it's your greatest strength. Treat yourself with the same kindness you would extend to a dear friend. Reflect on how you've learned, evolved, and become more aware through your experiences.

Remember, forgiving yourself doesn't mean forgetting or condoning mistakes; it's about releasing their hold on your heart, and letting go grants you freedom to move forward, unburdened by the past.

Replace self-criticism with gentle encouragement. When the whispers of doubt arise, challenge them with affirmations that resonate with your spirit. Embrace the healing power of positive self-talk, and watch how it transforms your perception of yourself.

You are worthy of love, especially your own. Embrace your humanness—flaws and all—as a part of your beautiful tapestry. In moments of self-doubt, remind yourself that you are evolving, growing, and deserving of kindness.

As you journey forward, remember that self-forgiveness is an ongoing practice. Be patient with yourself. Embrace the mistakes as catalysts for growth, and relish that you are constantly evolving into a stronger, wiser version of yourself.

With utmost compassion,

[Your Name]

Meditative Thought of the Day

In the tapestry of my journey, forgiveness has mended the threads of my past mistakes. The weight of regret has lifted, and a new dawn of understanding emerges. Each step forward celebrates growth, a testament to my resilience.

I embrace the lessons learned, transforming them into stepping stones towards a brighter future. With grace as my guide, I navigate life's path with a lighter heart, liberated from the shackles of self-condemnation.

The past no longer defines me; it's a chapter that enriches my story. In this newfound freedom, I nurture self-compassion, savoring the present moment and creating a canvas of possibility.

As the echoes of forgiveness resound, I revel in the beauty of imperfection, knowing that within my scars lies a journey of strength and wisdom.

Deeper Connection Within

1. Can you identify patterns or themes hindering your capacity to offer or receive forgiveness? How might they connect to your early experiences?

_____

_____

_____

_____

_____

2. In what ways might the process of forgiveness catalyze transforming your relationship with the past and creating a more harmonious present and future?

_____

_____

_____

_____

_____

3. What do your internal conversations look like when you engage in negative self-talk? How do these conversations impact your emotions and behaviors?

_____

_____

_____

_____

_____

Loving Statements About Me

My heart is open to forgiveness, and I release the grip of past hurts.

With each act of forgiveness, I liberate myself from the past's hold on me.

I am worthy of self-confidence, and I trust in my abilities to overcome challenges.

Gratitude Reflection of the Day

I appreciate the moments when I've shown kindness to myself, understanding that forgiveness begins within.

Inner Reflections

Overcome The Struggle To Forgive Your Inner Child

Forgiveness Reflection of the Day

Dear Me,

Take a moment to journey back into the recesses of your heart, where your inner child resides. As you read these words, remember that the child within you is a part of who you are today—an innocent soul who experienced joy and pain. It's time to extend a hand of understanding, forgiveness, and connection to that precious part of yourself.

Your inner child carries memories and emotions that have shaped your path. Embrace those memories, no matter how tender, for they hold the keys to your healing and growth. Acknowledge the hurts, the fears, and the unspoken desires. Hold them gently, like fragile treasures.

Know that you are not responsible for the pain your inner child experienced. Let go of any self-blame or resentment. Instead, offer the gift of self-compassion. Embrace your inner child with open arms like you would hold a beloved friend.

This journey is an act of restoration and healing. It's about weaving the threads of your past into a tapestry of strength. The wounds of yesterday can be transformed into the wisdom of today. Embrace the lessons learned, for they are the foundation for your future.

Connect deeply with your inner child, like an older sibling offering guidance and reassurance. Nurture your inner child's dreams, encouraging them to grow alongside your aspirations. Let your past be a source of inspiration, a reservoir of resilience.

Remember, this is not a one-time task but an ongoing practice. When old wounds resurface, hold them with tenderness, acknowledging their presence without judgment. Allow yourself to feel, to heal, and to grow.

As you move forward, let your inner child guide you. Embrace the wonder, curiosity, and boundless imagination that reside within you. With each step, build a bridge between your past and your future, recognizing that healing is an act of self-love and empowerment.

With love and understanding,

[Your Name]

Meditative Thought of the Day

In the sacred space of self-discovery, I've bridged the gap to my inner child. Tender whispers of forgiveness have woven a tapestry of healing between us. With each step, laughter's melody resonates, a reminder of innocence embraced. The wounds of the past transform into a garden of resilience tended with self-love.

Through forgiveness, I've cradled my inner child, dispelling shadows of pain. Together, we dance in the sunlight of acceptance, a symphony of connection and joy. I relish the magic of simple moments, reclaiming lost dreams and nurturing creativity. In this reunion, authenticity reigns, and the song of my heart flows freely. The past's grip has loosened, and as I hold my inner child's hand, I walk toward wholeness.

The journey continues hand in hand, celebrating reunion and an ode to the beauty of forgiveness.

Deeper Connection Within

1. Can you trace the origins of these negative self-talk patterns back to specific events, people, or beliefs? How do they continue to influence your self-perception?

_____

_____

_____

_____

2. How might the words you use when speaking to yourself echo the language or attitudes you absorbed from others during your upbringing?

_____

_____

_____

_____

3. What aspects of your self-worth and identity are most affected by negative self-talk? How can you reshape these aspects with self-compassionate dialogue?

_____

_____

_____

_____

Loving Statements About Me

My self-confidence grows stronger as I recognize my unique strengths.

I believe in myself and my capacity to face any obstacle with courage.

With every step I take, my self-confidence deepens, shaping my journey.

Gratitude Reflection of the Day

I'm thankful for the capacity to forgive others, as it frees me from the burden of resentment and anger.

Inner Reflections

Overcome The Struggle To Forgive Your Body

Forgiveness Reflection of the Day

Dear Me,

In this moment of reflection, I want you to understand that your body is a sacred vessel that carries your spirit, dreams, and potential. As you read these words, let them remind you that it's time to release the weight of body shaming and embrace the beauty of self-love and accountability.

Your body has been with you through every triumph and challenge, a faithful companion on this life journey. Let go of the hurtful words you've directed towards it and replace them with kindness and appreciation. Treat your body as you would a cherished friend—with love, respect, and care.

Embrace the truth that your body is not your enemy; it's your ally. It's a canvas that tells the story of your experiences, a testament to your resilience and strength. Let go of comparisons and unrealistic expectations. Your body is unique, and that's where its beauty lies.

While loving your body is essential, so is being accountable for your health and lifestyle choices. Nourish your body with wholesome foods, engage in joyful movement, and cultivate habits that promote overall well-being. This isn't about conforming to societal standards but honoring yourself.

Remember, healing isn't just about the physical; it's about nurturing your mind and soul. Embrace practices that bring you joy, peace, and clarity. Forgive yourself for any past neglect, and embrace this opportunity to embark on a holistic journey towards health.

Let this be a lifelong commitment—to love, nurture, and care for yourself. When you look in the mirror, let the reflection remind you of your worthiness, strength, and beauty—inside and out.

As you move forward, remember that every choice you make is an act of self-love and self-respect. Your body is a temple, and you are the guardian of its well-being. Embrace the journey with an open heart, knowing that healing is a gift you give yourself.

With unwavering support and love,

[Your Name]

Meditative Thought of the Day

Through the labyrinth of self-acceptance, I've embraced a profound connection with my body. Forgiveness has woven a tapestry of compassion, healing the wounds of self-judgment. With each breath, a symphony of gratitude resounds, celebrating my body's resilience and grace.

I've shed the weight of criticism, finding beauty in every curve, scar, and imperfection. In this newfound harmony, I move with intention, honoring the vessel that carries my spirit. The mirror reflects a story of strength, endurance, and growth.

With forgiveness as my compass, I navigate a path of self-care, cultivating a sanctuary of vitality. The whispers of self-love mend old wounds, replacing them with a tapestry of acceptance. In this sacred dance between body and soul, I am reborn, liberated from the chains of discontent.

The journey towards healing continues, a testament to the beauty of forgiveness and the celebration of self.

Deeper Connection Within

1. How might your journey toward self-forgiveness intertwine your efforts to replace negative self-talk with empowering and uplifting affirmations?

_____

_____

_____

_____

_____

2. Can you recall instances from your past that planted the seeds of guilt and shame within you? How have they taken root in your psyche over time?

_____

_____

_____

_____

_____

3. How do daily guilt and shame affect your relationships, decisions, and overall well-being?

_____

_____

_____

_____

_____

Loving Statements About Me

Self-confidence is my armor against doubt, and I wear it proudly.

I trust my instincts and follow my heart's guidance on my journey.

Inner trust is my compass, leading to decisions aligned with my purpose.

Gratitude Reflection of the Day

I appreciate when I've nurtured loving energy, allowing it to radiate toward those around me.

Inner Reflections

Overcome Your Struggle To Forgive Your Limiting Thoughts

Forgiveness Reflection of the Day

Dear Me,

Pause for a moment and listen to the whispers of your heart. As you read these words, know you can rewrite the narrative that holds you back. It's time to release the grip of limiting thoughts and embrace the boundless potential within you.

The thoughts that once whispered doubt and insecurity are not your truth. Let go of the "I'm not good enough" and "I can't" narratives. Replace them with declarations of empowerment and possibility. You are more than enough and possess the strength to conquer challenges.

Embrace the idea that your age, appearance, or other perceived limitations are not defining factors. Your uniqueness is your strength, and your journey is a testament to your resilience. Embrace every step, knowing that each one leads to growth.

Banish the fear of failure and replace it with curiosity. What if you succeed beyond your wildest dreams? What if you uncover talents and passions you never knew existed? Trust in your ability to learn, adapt, and thrive.

The words "not smart enough" or "not creative enough" no longer hold power over you. Embrace the truth that creativity and intelligence are not finite resources. Embrace your innate curiosity, and know that growth comes through exploration and learning.

Embrace your limitless potential with unwavering belief. Every obstacle you face is an opportunity for growth. Look beyond the horizon of your doubts to the realm of infinite possibilities. You have the power to shape your reality.

As you journey forward, let your thoughts be a chorus of empowerment. Speak words that uplift, inspire, and motivate. Cultivate self-belief, and watch how it transforms your perception of what's achievable.

Remember, this is a continuous practice. When limiting thoughts arise, challenge them with evidence of your accomplishments, strengths, and aspirations. The path to empowerment is paved with self-compassion, courage, and a willingness to rewrite your story.

Embrace your potential, embrace your worthiness, and step into a world of limitless outcomes. Your journey is a testament to your ability to rise above self-imposed boundaries.

With boundless support and belief,

[Your Name]

Meditative Thought of the Day

In the realm of transformation, I've shattered the chains of limiting thoughts and beliefs. Forgiveness has kindled a fire within, burning away self-doubt's grip. With each idea redirected, a symphony of empowerment resonates, celebrating my boundless potential.

The shackles of old narratives crumble, replaced by affirmations of possibility and growth. In this awakening, I embrace the power to rewrite my story, reclaiming my dreams with unwavering faith.

With forgiveness as my guide, I navigate a journey of self-discovery, cultivating a garden of positivity. The echoes of self-love drown out the whispers of inadequacy, birthing a tapestry of resilience. Amid the tapestry of transformation, I rise, renewed by the beauty of self-forgiveness.

The journey continues, a dance of liberation and empowerment, a testament to the infinite possibilities that unfold when limiting beliefs are released.

Deeper Connection Within

1. What self-perceptions and narratives do you hold about yourself due to guilt and shame? How do they contribute to your emotional burden?

_____

_____

_____

_____

_____

2. Can you identify any instances where your actions were misinterpreted by you or others, leading to unwarranted guilt or shame?

_____

_____

_____

_____

_____

3. How might releasing guilt and shame be essential to creating a new narrative for yourself—one rooted in self-acceptance, self-love, and personal growth?

_____

_____

_____

_____

_____

Loving Statements About Me

I navigate life's twists and turns with grace and certainty as I trust myself.

My inner trust is unshakable, allowing me to face uncertainty with confidence.

The more I trust myself, the more I create a life that resonates with my soul.

Gratitude Reflection of the Day

Today, I'm sending kind and forgiving thoughts to those who may have hurt me. It's a step towards releasing the weight of past grievances.

Inner Reflections

Overcome Your Struggle To Forgive Career Choices

Forgiveness Reflection of the Day

Dear Me,

In this moment of self-reflection, I want you to understand that your career journey is a series of stepping stones, each contributing to the remarkable person you are today. As you read these words, know it's time to release the weight of regret and embrace the power of forgiveness and proactive change.

Your past career choices have shaped you, but they don't define your future. Let go of the "should haves" and "could haves." Instead, focus on the present moment—a canvas where you can paint your desired future. You can redirect your path towards the person you aspire to be.

It's time to release self-judgment and replace it with self-empowerment. Your career journey is a tapestry woven with lessons and experiences that have honed your skills and insights. Embrace your strengths and build on them, recognizing that you can grow.

Remember, taking action is critical. Progress requires steps, whether they're small or bold. Let go of the fear of change and take meaningful strides towards your aspirations. You can shape your career path one decision at a time.

Embrace the mindset of learning and adaptation. Your journey is not linear, and pivoting and exploring new avenues is okay. Instead of dwelling on past choices, channel your energy into crafting a vision for your future self.

As you progress, remember that your career is a journey of self-discovery and evolution. Each moment is an opportunity to take control of your narrative. Surround yourself with positive influences, seek mentorship, and gather knowledge that propels you forward.

Forgive yourself for any perceived missteps, for they are the stepping stones that have led you to this point of growth and transformation. Embrace the journey with an open heart and a willingness to embrace change.

With determination and self-belief,

[Your Name]

Meditative Thought of the Day

In the sanctuary of self-discovery, I've unlocked the door to forgiveness for my career choices and inaction. Compassion has woven a tapestry of understanding, dispelling the shadows of regret. With each step forward, a symphony of empowerment resounds, a celebration of my capacity to create change.

The weight of past decisions has lifted, replaced by the lightness of newfound purpose. In this rebirth, I embrace the power to chart a new course fueled by lessons learned and courage ignited. I navigate a growth path with forgiveness as my compass, forging a destiny that aligns with my aspirations.

The whispers of self-belief drown out the echoes of doubt, creating a tapestry of resilience and possibility. Amidst the tapestry of transformation, I rise, triumphant in the beauty of self-forgiveness.

The journey continues an exploration of progress and self-realization, a testament to the boundless horizons that open when forgiveness paves the way.

Deeper Connection Within

1. How do you experience the call for healing from your heart? What sensations, emotions, or insights arise when you approach your struggles from a heart-centered perspective?

_____

_____

_____

_____

_____

2. Can you recall a moment where you felt a profound heart-centered shift in your perception, leading to deeper understanding or forgiveness?

_____

_____

_____

_____

_____

3. What activities or practices connect you with your heart's wisdom and intuition? How can you integrate them into your healing journey?

_____

_____

_____

_____

_____

Loving Statements About Me

I accept myself fully, embracing every aspect of myself, flaws and all.

Through self-acceptance, I liberate myself from the burden of perfectionism.

I release the need to meet others' expectations and embrace my authentic self.

Gratitude Reflection of the Day

I'm grateful for the awareness that forgiveness is a gift I give to myself, allowing me to find inner peace and serenity.

Inner Reflections

DAY 7

Overcome The Struggle To Forgive Your Partner

Forgiveness Reflection of the Day

Dear Me,

As you read these words, let the light of understanding and compassion fill your heart. It's time to release the grip of judgment and embrace the beauty of forgiveness and appreciation for your partner. Remember, they are complex, like you, with strengths and imperfections.

Let go of the lens of criticism and replace it with empathy. Your partner, like you, is on a journey of growth and self-discovery. Embrace their uniqueness and recognize the qualities that drew you to them in the first place.

Shift your focus from their flaws to their virtues. Remember the moments of laughter, shared dreams, and unconditional support. See the greatness within them—their kindness, resilience, and the love they bring into your life.

Recognize that they deserve the same just as you seek understanding and forgiveness. Open your heart to their perspective, and engage in open and compassionate communication. Let go of the need to be right instead of striving for connection and mutual growth.

Forgiveness doesn't mean condoning hurtful actions; it means releasing their hold on your heart. It's about making space for healing and fostering a stronger, more loving bond. As you forgive, you free yourself from the weight of resentment.

Remember that relationships are a dance of mutual learning and growth. Each partner brings their strengths and areas of development. Embrace this journey as an opportunity for both of you to evolve and thrive.

Let your heart be a sanctuary of understanding and grace as you move forward. Celebrate the moments of joy, support, and companionship. Choose to see the greatness in your partner and watch how it transforms your relationship into a haven of love and connection.

With love and compassion,

[Your Name]

Meditative Celebration Thought of the Day

In the sanctuary of my heart, I've unfurled the wings of forgiveness towards my partner. Compassion has stitched a tapestry of healing, weaving threads of understanding and empathy. With each moment of connection, a symphony of love resounds, celebrating our shared journey and growth.

The burdens of resentment have melted away, replaced by the lightness of renewal and reconciliation. In this rekindling, I embrace the power to nurture trust, to mend what was once fractured. With forgiveness as my guiding star, I navigate a path of unity, recognizing that our imperfections are the canvas of our shared story.

The whispers of acceptance eclipse the echoes of discord, crafting a tapestry of resilience and harmony. Amidst the tapestry of togetherness, we rise, triumphant in the beauty of forgiveness.

The journey continues an exploration of love and evolution, a testament to the depth of connection that flourishes when forgiveness becomes the bridge.

Deeper Connection Within

1. How might allowing your heart to guide you help you access suppressed emotions, release emotional pain, and promote self-forgiveness?

_____

_____

_____

_____

_____

2. What kind of space and environment can you create to support you in nurturing your heart and fostering profound healing?

_____

_____

_____

_____

_____

3. Reflect on your beliefs about forgiveness, self-worth, and healing capacity. How have these beliefs formed, and how do they affect your actions?

_____

_____

_____

_____

_____

Loving Statements About Me

My self-acceptance paves the way for deeper connections and understanding.

Acceptance of myself radiates acceptance of others, creating harmony in my life.

Joy flows freely through me, nourishing my spirit and guiding my actions.

Gratitude Reflection of the Day

I appreciate the moments of clarity when I've let go of grudges and embraced a more compassionate outlook.

Inner Reflections

Overcome Your Struggle To Forgive Siblings

Forgiveness Reflection of the Day

Dear Me,

In self-discovery, let the echoes of understanding and healing resonate within you. It's time to unburden yourself from the weight of unforgiveness and create space for reconciliation and restored connections with your siblings. Remember, your bond is rooted in shared experiences and a shared journey.

Release the grip of resentment and embrace the power of forgiveness. Let go of past hurts, acknowledging that growth and change are possible for everyone, including your siblings. By forgiving, you liberate yourself from the chains of bitterness and pain.

Rebuilding relationships doesn't mean abandoning your boundaries; it means setting healthy ones that foster respect and understanding. Communicate your needs and expectations openly, creating an environment of mutual consideration and growth.

Strive for open and empathetic communication. Listen as much as you express, understanding that each sibling has a unique perspective. Engage in conversations that nourish connection rather than reinforce distance.

Remember, siblings are a part of your journey—individuals with their paths, struggles, and aspirations. Embrace the beauty of shared memories and the potential for creating new ones together. Focus on the positive qualities that make your sibling relationships unique.

Let your heart be a space of forgiveness and understanding as you move forward. Choose to release the weight of the past and embrace the potential for a renewed bond. By rebuilding bridges, you contribute to the tapestry of love, growth, and unity within your family.

With love and healing intent,

[Your Name]

Meditative Thought of the Day

In embracing inner peace, I've journeyed to forgive my siblings. Compassion has woven a tapestry of understanding, stitching wounds with threads of empathy. A symphony of unity resonates with each shared memory, celebrating our shared bond and growth.

The weight of past conflicts has dissolved, replaced by the warmth of restored connections. In this reunion, I embrace the power to build bridges, let go of grievances, and foster newfound harmony.

With forgiveness as my compass, I navigate a path of reconciliation, realizing that our differences add depth to our shared tapestry—the whispers of acceptance silence the echoes of discord, weaving a tapestry of resilience and love.

Amidst the tapestry of familial bonds, we rise, triumphant in the beauty of forgiveness. The journey continues an exploration of love and growth, a testament to the strength of kinship that flourishes when forgiveness is nurtured.

Deeper Connection Within

1. Can you recall moments when you've witnessed or experienced forgiveness in a transformative way? How do these instances challenge or support your own beliefs?

_____

_____

_____

_____

_____

2. How do your beliefs align with cultural, societal, or familial expectations? How have these external influences shaped your self-perception and struggles?

_____

_____

_____

_____

_____

3. What stories and narratives do you tell yourself about your past, and how might they perpetuate feelings of guilt, shame, or negative self-talk?

_____

_____

_____

_____

_____

Loving Statements About Me

I choose to focus on the beauty and positivity in every situation.

As I release past grievances, I invite harmony to reign in my heart and relationships.

My heart is a vessel of joy, and I spread its radiance wherever I go.

Gratitude Reflection of the Day

I'm thankful for the strength within me to forgive, even when it's challenging, as it leads me closer to inner harmony.

Inner Reflections

Overcome The Struggle To Forgive Your Children

Forgiveness Reflection of the Day

Dear Me,

In the realm of parenthood, let the waves of love and understanding wash over you. It's time to release the hold of resentment and create a space of forgiveness and nurturing energy for your children. Remember, your journey as a parent is a tapestry woven with challenges and growth.

Let go of the weight of past frustrations and disappointments. Embrace the power of forgiveness, not only for your children but also for yourself. By forgiving, you free yourself from negative emotions, creating room for healing and renewal.

Forgiveness doesn't mean condoning every action but letting go of the emotional burden. Understand that your children are navigating their paths, learning, and growing. Embrace their uniqueness and their potential to change.

Cultivate healthy habits of communication and understanding. Open your heart to their perspectives, even if they differ from your own. Practice active listening and empathy, fostering an environment of mutual respect.

Remember that your children are on their journeys with their dreams, fears, and challenges. Let your love guide them, offering support and guidance while allowing them to explore and learn. Be a source of strength and unwavering belief.

As you move forward, let your heart radiate love and understanding. Set an example of self-compassion, showing them that it's okay to make mistakes and to forgive. Embrace the moments of connection, laughter, and shared growth.

Nurture the bond with your children, building a foundation of trust and unconditional love. Be patient with their growth and your journey as a parent. You develop a loving and supportive family environment by forgiving and fostering positive energy.

With love and nurturing intent,

[Your Name]

Meditative Thought of the Day

In the sanctuary of my heart, I've woven the tapestry of forgiveness towards my children. Compassion has etched a path of understanding, bridging gaps with threads of unconditional love. With each shared moment, a symphony of connection resounds a celebration of our evolving relationship and shared growth.

The weight of past misunderstandings has lifted, replaced by the grace of renewed bonds. In this embrace, I cherish the power to nurture trust, mend, and create anew. With forgiveness as my guiding light, I navigate a path of unity, recognizing that growth often emerges from challenges. The whispers of acceptance drown out the echoes of discord, crafting a tapestry of resilience and devotion.

Amidst the tapestry of family ties, we rise, triumphant in the beauty of forgiveness. The journey explores love's transformative power, a testament to the profound depth that blooms when forgiveness is embraced.

Deeper Connection Within

1. How can you initiate a process of challenging and reframing your beliefs to create a fertile ground for forgiveness, self-compassion, and personal growth?

----

2. Reflect on moments of self-compassion and self-love you've experienced. What situations or practices evoke these feelings, and how do they impact your well-being?

----

3. Can you recall instances when you've extended compassion and love to others who faced challenges similar to yours? How can you extend the same to yourself?

Loving Statements About Me

Through forgiveness and self-love, I restore the harmonious balance within me.

I love myself unconditionally, recognizing my worthiness of love and care.

Self-love is my foundation for meaningful connections and personal growth.

Gratitude Reflection of the Day

Today, I'm sending thoughts of forgiveness to anyone I may have unintentionally harmed. We are all on a journey of growth.

Inner Reflections

Overcome Your Struggle To Forgive Women

Forgiveness Reflection of the Day

Dear Me,

As you embark on the journey of healing and growth, let the echoes of compassion and understanding guide your path. It's time to release the weight of pain and resentment carried from both conscious and subconscious hurts caused by women. Remember, like all individuals, women have complexities and struggles that shape their actions.

Forgiveness is not a sign of weakness; it's a courageous act of liberation. Let go of the grip of resentment, acknowledging that holding onto hurt only binds you to the past. By forgiving, you break the chains that keep you from embracing joy and healing.

Understand that conscious or subconscious hurt often reflects one's pain. By forgiving, you allow yourself to rise above the cycle of hurt and retaliation. Choose to transcend negativity and embrace the power of empathy.

Release the expectations you may have placed on women, and instead, focus on the qualities that unite us all—our capacity for growth, understanding, and connection. Embrace the shared experiences and aspirations that transcend differences.

Forgiveness doesn't mean forgetting or allowing mistreatment; it means letting it no longer define your emotions. You can release the pain and create space for positivity and healing.

As you move forward, let your heart be a sanctuary of healing and empathy. Replace judgment with understanding and resentment with compassion. Choose to see the goodness within every woman, recognizing that we are all navigating life's challenges and striving for growth.

Your journey towards forgiveness is a step towards your liberation. Embrace the power of forgiveness to shape a brighter, more positive future free from the chains of hurt and negativity.

With love and healing intent,

[Your Name]

Meditative Thought of the Day

In the haven of self-discovery, I've unfurled the flag of forgiveness for women, releasing conscious and hidden hurts. Compassion has woven a tapestry of empathy, threading connections beyond pain. A symphony of sisterhood resounds with each shared understanding, celebrating unity and growth.

The weight of past wounds has dissolved, making space for the radiance of healing connections. In this embrace, I can transcend pain, break cycles, and build bridges of genuine empathy. With forgiveness as my compass, I navigate a path of mutual support, recognizing that each encounter is an opportunity for healing and transformation.

The whispers of unity eclipse the echoes of division, crafting a tapestry of resilience and solidarity. Amidst the tapestry of shared experiences, we rise, triumphant in the beauty of forgiveness. The journey continues, an exploration of empowerment and collaboration, a testament to the strength that flourishes when understanding and forgiveness unite.

Deeper Connection Within

1. How might your understanding of compassion and self-love shift as you explore their role in your journey toward self-forgiveness?

_____

_____

_____

_____

_____

2. Reflect on treating yourself as you would a dear friend. How might this practice guide your self-talk, decisions, and overall self-perception?

_____

_____

_____

_____

_____

3. What steps can you take to cultivate a genuine, consistent practice of self-compassion and self-love that counteracts feelings of guilt and shame?

_____

_____

_____

_____

_____

Loving Statements About Me

With each act of self-love, I create a wellspring of compassion within me.

My self-love is a beacon that attracts positivity and abundance into my life.

I shower with love, knowing it's the key to a fulfilling life.

Gratitude Reflection of the Day

I appreciate the power of forgiveness to mend relationships and bring about positive change.

Inner Reflections

Overcome The Struggle To Forgive Your Current Partner

Forgiveness Reflection of the Day

Dear Me,

In the realm of love and understanding, let the warmth of healing and growth envelop you. It's time to release the hold of resentment and open your heart to forgiveness, allowing the restoration of loving energy and happy thoughts with your current partner. Remember, your relationship is a journey of shared experiences and mutual growth.

Let go of the weight of past disagreements and hurts. Embrace the power of forgiveness, not only for your partner but also for yourself. By forgiving, you unburden yourself from the chains of negativity and create space for healing and reconnection.

Forgiveness isn't a declaration of defeat; it's a choice to prioritize your relationship over past grievances. Understand that you and your partner are evolving beings with your strengths and growth areas. Choose to see the potential for positive change.

Rekindle the spark of love by fostering open and honest communication. Engage in conversations that nurture understanding and unity. Release the urge to hold onto past hurts and instead focus on building a future rooted in shared dreams and aspirations.

Remember that your partner is not your adversary; they are your ally in this journey of love. Embrace the qualities that drew you to them in the first place, and choose to see their efforts to make the relationship flourish.

As you move forward, let your heart be a sanctuary of healing and renewal. Replace resentment with empathy and frustration with patience. Embrace the joy, laughter, and shared connection moments that have made your relationship special.

Nurture the bond with your partner, sowing seeds of love and understanding. Choose to see their potential, and watch how it transforms your relationship into a haven of love and harmony. By forgiving and moving forward, you contribute to the growth of a stronger and more connected partnership.

With love and rekindled intent,

[Your Name]

Meditative Thought of the Day

In the sanctuary of my heart, I've unveiled the treasure of forgiveness for my current partner. Compassion has woven a tapestry of understanding, stitching together our shared journey with threads of empathy. With each moment of connection, a symphony of love resounds, celebrating our growth and the beauty of companionship.

The burdens of past conflicts have dissolved, replaced by the lightness of renewed love and trust. In this union, I embrace the power to heal wounds, to nurture what was once strained. With forgiveness as my guiding light, I navigate a path of harmony, realizing that our imperfections only enrich our shared tapestry.

The whispers of acceptance quiet the echoes of discord, weaving a tapestry of resilience and unity. Amidst the tapestry of our partnership, we rise, triumphant in the beauty of forgiveness. The journey explores love's depths, a testament to the strength of a bond that flourishes when forgiveness becomes a bridge.

Deeper Connection Within

1. Reflect on instances where vulnerability has led to growth, understanding, or connection in your life. How can you apply these positive experiences to your struggles?

_____

_____

_____

_____

_____

2. How has the fear of being vulnerable influenced your approach to forgiving yourself, forgiving others, and addressing negative self-talk?

_____

_____

_____

_____

_____

3. Can you identify any common fears associated with vulnerability in the context of your journey? How might you address and challenge these fears?

_____

_____

_____

_____

_____

Loving Statements About Me

The past no longer defines me; I release its grip and move forward.

I free myself from the shackles of past mistakes, embracing the present moment.

Each day is a fresh start, and I release the past with gratitude for its lessons.

Gratitude Reflection of the Day

I'm grateful for the moments when I've chosen forgiveness over resentment, recognizing the healing it brings.

Inner Reflections

DAY 12

Overcome Your Struggle To Forgive Ex-Partners

Forgiveness Reflection of the Day

Dear Me,

In the realm of healing and growth, let the gentle winds of understanding and compassion guide you. It's time to release the grip of past hurt and resentment towards your ex-partners and open your heart to forgiveness, allowing healing energy to flow. Remember, every relationship is a chapter of your journey, and each ex-partner has shaped who you are today.

Let go of the weight of misunderstandings and wounds. Embrace the power of forgiveness, not for their sake, but for your liberation. By forgiving, you free yourself from negativity and make room for healing and renewal.

Forgiveness doesn't mean forgetting the past; it means releasing its hold on your present and future. Understand that misunderstandings and hurt are part of the human experience. By forgiving, you remove the power these memories have over you.

Embrace the notion that healing begins within. Redirect your energy from resentment to self-compassion. Recognize that you are deserving of peace and happiness and that forgiving your ex-partners is an act of self-love.

Release the need to carry past grievances; channel that energy toward your growth and well-being. Use the lessons learned from these relationships to shape your journey toward greater self-awareness and self-love.

Remember, forgiveness is a process that takes time. Allow yourself to grieve, to heal, and to release. Replace bitterness with empathy and pain with understanding. Embrace the potential for healing energy to flow through your heart, creating a space for love and renewal.

As you move forward, let your heart be a sanctuary of healing and growth. Replace old wounds with the potential for new beginnings. Choose to see the beauty in the lessons learned from your past relationships, and watch how they guide you towards a future of self-discovery and empowerment.

With love and healing intent,

[Your Name]

Meditative Thought of the Day

In the sanctuary of self-discovery, I've unfurled the flag of forgiveness for my ex-partners. Compassion has woven a tapestry of understanding, threading connections beyond heartache. With each moment of closure, a symphony of release resounds, a celebration of liberation and growth.

The weight of past relationships has lifted, making space for the lightness of self-renewal. In this embrace, I hold the power to heal old wounds, to grant myself the grace to move forward. With forgiveness as my guiding star, I navigate a path of self-empowerment, recognizing that each relationship has shaped my journey. The whispers of self-love eclipse the echoes of pain, crafting a tapestry of resilience and self-discovery. Amidst the tapestry of life lessons, I rise, triumphant in the beauty of forgiveness.

The journey continues an exploration of self-evolution, a testament to the strength that flourishes when the past's weight is released.

Deeper Connection Within

1. Reflect on the concept of "radical vulnerability." What might it mean to fully embrace your authentic self, even when it feels uncomfortable?

_____

_____

_____

_____

_____

2. How might embracing vulnerability be a key component in dismantling the layers of guilt, shame, and self-criticism that hold you back?

_____

_____

_____

_____

_____

3. Reflect on the influences contributing to your perspective on forgiveness, self-worth, and guilt. How have these external sources shaped your internal dialogue?

_____

_____

_____

_____

_____

Loving Statements About Me

My history does not bind me; my current choices empower me.

The past has shaped me, but I decide my future with every new step.

I am the author of my story, and I reclaim my power to shape my narrative.

Gratitude Reflection of the Day

I appreciate the joy and lightness that forgiveness brings to my heart and soul.

Inner Reflections

Overcome Your Struggle To Forgive Friends

Forgiveness Reflection of the Day

Dear Me,

Amid the tapestry of life's relationships, let the rays of understanding and healing guide your path. It's time to release the grip of resentment and open your heart to forgiveness, allowing the restoration of your inner strength and faith in friendship. Friendships are journeys of shared experiences, growth, and mutual support.

Let go of the weight of past disappointments and hurt. Embrace the power of forgiveness, not only for your friends but also for your well-being. By forgiving, you liberate yourself from negativity and make room for healing and reconnection.

Understand that friends like you are human, with their struggles and imperfections. Release the need for perfection and embrace the diversity that makes each friendship unique. Choose to see the good intentions that misunderstandings may have overshadowed.

Foster open and honest communication with your friends. Engage in conversations that allow you to express your feelings while listening to their perspective. Release the urge to hold onto grudges, and instead, focus on the shared history and positive qualities that drew you together.

Remember that friendships are built on mutual growth and support. Your friends, like you, are on their journeys. Choose to see their efforts, intentions, laughter, and shared moments that have enriched your life.

As you move forward, let your heart be a sanctuary of understanding and resilience. Replace resentment with empathy and hurt with courage. Embrace the moments of connection, support, and shared experiences that have made your friendships special.

Nurture the bonds with your friends, sowing seeds of forgiveness and understanding. Choose to see the potential for renewal and growth within these relationships. By forgiving and moving forward, you contribute to a future filled with strengthened friendships and a deeper appreciation for those who uplift and enrich your life.

With love and friendship in your heart,

[Your Name]

Meditative Thought of the Day

In the sanctuary of my heart, I've embraced the essence of forgiveness for my friends. Compassion has woven a tapestry of understanding, threading connections beyond misunderstandings.

A symphony of friendship resounds with each shared laughter, celebrating growth and shared experiences. The weight of past grievances has dissolved, replaced by the warmth of rekindled bonds. In this reunion, I cherish the power to mend, to build anew on the foundation of cherished memories. With forgiveness as my guiding light, I navigate a path of renewal, recognizing that friendships are a testament to our capacity to evolve.

The whispers of acceptance quiet the echoes of resentment, weaving a tapestry of resilience and connection. Amidst the tapestry of companionship, we rise, triumphant in the beauty of forgiveness. The journey continues, exploring mutual support and authenticity, a testament to the strength that flourishes when understanding and forgiveness reign.

Deeper Connection Within

1. Can you identify individuals or relationships perpetuating your struggles with forgiveness, negative self-talk, guilt, or shame?

_____

_____

_____

_____

_____

2. How do societal norms and cultural expectations impact how you perceive forgiveness and self-worth? How do they relate to your struggles?

_____

_____

_____

_____

_____

3. Reflect on instances where you've internalized the opinions or judgments of others. How can you disentangle these external voices from your inner truth?

_____

_____

_____

_____

_____

Loving Statements About Me

External opinions hold no dominion over my self-worth and decisions.

My strength comes from within, and I trust my ability to overcome challenges.

I control my reactions, emotions, and the direction of my life.

Gratitude Reflection of the Day

I'm thankful for the lessons I've learned through forgiveness—lessons of compassion, empathy, and resilience.

Inner Reflections

Overcome Your Struggle To Forgive God

Forgiveness Reflection of the Day

Dear Me,

Amidst the ebb and flow of life's journey, let the gentle winds of understanding and healing carry you. It's time to release the weight of hurt and confusion and open your heart to forgiveness, allowing the restoration of your faith, trust, and friendship with the divine. Remember, your connection with the divine is a sacred bond that can weather even the storms of doubt.

Let go of the pain and questions that have burdened your heart. Embrace the power of forgiveness, not because the divine needs it, but because you do. By forgiving, you free yourself from resentment and open the door to healing and renewing your spiritual connection.

Understand that your struggles and questions are part of your journey towards more profound understanding. Release the need for immediate answers and embrace the mystery of life's challenges.

Know that your relationship with the divine is not one-sided; it's a dialogue of seeking and receiving.

Foster an open-hearted conversation with the divine. Share your doubts, your frustrations, and your pain. Release the notion that you must have all the answers, and instead, trust that your journey is unfolding as it should. Choose to see the divine's presence in the small moments of beauty and grace.

Remember that your connection with the divine is an evolving friendship. Just as friends support you through both joys and trials, the divine stands beside you on your path. Choose to see the divine's intentions of growth, love, and guidance, even in the midst of challenges.

As you move forward, let your heart be a sanctuary of trust and restoration. Replace doubt with curiosity and pain with surrender. Embrace the moments of connection, inner peace, and inspired insights that have strengthened your bond with the divine.

Nurture your friendship with the divine, sowing seeds of understanding and faith. Choose to see the divine's wisdom in the weaving of your story. By forgiving and embracing this spiritual relationship, you create a space for healing, growth, and a deeper connection to the source of all love and light.

With love and renewed faith,

[Your Name]

Meditative Thought of the Day

In the sanctuary of my spirit, I've embraced the profound journey of forgiving God. Compassion has woven a tapestry of understanding, threading my connection beyond the shadows of confusion.

With each moment of surrender, a symphony of faith resounds, a celebration of growth and spiritual renewal. The weight of questions and struggles has dissolved, making space for the light of trust and acceptance. In this surrender, I embrace the power to release doubts and navigate life's labyrinth with newfound serenity. With forgiveness as my guiding light, I navigate a path of spiritual harmony, recognizing that our divine journey is woven with mysteries.

The whispers of surrender eclipse the echoes of resistance, crafting a tapestry of resilience and faith. Amidst the tapestry of spiritual evolution, I rise, triumphant in the beauty of forgiveness. The journey continues an exploration of divine connection, a testament to the strength that flourishes when the heart opens to embrace the divine plan.

Deeper Connection Within

1. How might fostering discernment and setting boundaries with external influences support your efforts to release guilt, shame, and negative self-talk?

_____

_____

_____

_____

_____

2. Reflect on your early childhood experiences. Are there moments where you felt guilty, ashamed, or undeserving? How have these moments shaped your self-perception?

_____

_____

_____

_____

_____

3. How might your inner child's perspective on forgiveness, negative self-talk, guilt, and shame influence your adult struggles in these areas?

_____

_____

_____

_____

_____

Loving Statements About Me

With each moment of empowerment, I reshape my reality and destiny.

The only opinion that truly matters about me is my own.

I release the need to seek validation from others; my worth is inherent.

Gratitude Reflection of the Day

Today, I'm sending loving energy to those who have forgiven me, acknowledging the beauty of their generosity.

Inner Reflections

Overcome Your Struggle To Forgive Bullies

Forgiveness Reflection of the Day

Dear Me,

Amid the journey of self-discovery, let the flames of empowerment and healing guide your path. It's time to release the grip of hurt and resentment caused by bullies and embrace the power of forgiveness, allowing your inner strength and unshakable confidence to emerge. Remember, you are a beacon of resilience and self-worth.

Let go of the weight of their hurtful words and actions. Embrace the power of forgiveness, not for their sake, but for yours. By forgiving, you free yourself from negativity and make room for healing and self-empowerment.

Understand that bullies often project their insecurities onto others. Release the need to internalize their opinions and instead embrace your uniqueness and the qualities that make you unique. Choose to see yourself through the lens of self-love.

Foster an inner dialogue that champions your worthiness. Replace the echoes of hurtful words with affirmations of strength, courage, and resilience. Remember that you deserve respect and kindness from others and yourself.

Recognize that forgiving bullies doesn't excuse their behavior; it frees you from their hold on your emotions. By forgiving, you reclaim your power and allow space for personal growth and healing.

As you move forward, let your heart be a sanctuary of self-love and empowerment. Replace self-doubt with self-confidence and pain with strength. Embrace the moments of courage and determination that have fortified your spirit.

Nurture your inner strength, sowing seeds of positivity and self-assurance. Choose to see yourself as a warrior who has faced challenges and emerged stronger. By forgiving and embracing your resilience, you unleash the potential to rise above negativity and shine brightly.

With unwavering support and empowerment,

[Your Name]

Meditative Thought of the Day

In the sanctuary of my soul, I've found the courage to forgive the bullies. Compassion has woven a tapestry of understanding, threading connections beyond hurtful actions. With each act of letting go, a symphony of healing resounds, celebrating liberation and growth.

The weight of past wounds has dissolved, replaced by the lightness of inner freedom. In this release, I can break the cycle of pain and transform adversity into strength. With forgiveness as my guiding star, I navigate a path of empowerment, realizing that the bullies' actions don't define me.

The whispers of self-worth eclipse the echoes of cruelty, weaving a tapestry of resilience and self-discovery. Amidst the tapestry of personal growth, I rise, triumphant in the beauty of forgiveness. The journey continues an exploration of strength and self-empowerment, a testament to the victory of love over hate.

Deeper Connection Within

1. How can you nurture your inner child and offer them the understanding, love, and validation they may not have received during challenging moments?

_____
_____
_____
_____
_____

2. Reflect on how your present choices and actions can provide the healing and support your inner child needed back then.

_____
_____
_____
_____
_____

3. How might addressing your inner child's needs pave the way for a more profound healing journey focused on self-forgiveness, self-acceptance, and self-love?

_____
_____
_____
_____
_____

Loving Statements About Me

The judgments of others do not define me; my inner truth guides me.

I embrace my uniqueness and relinquish the need to conform to external expectations.

I stand firm in my authenticity, immune to the opinions that seek to diminish me.

Gratitude Reflection of the Day

I appreciate the opportunities I have to practice forgiveness daily, for it is a skill that can transform lives.

Inner Reflections

Overcome Your Struggles With Money

Forgiveness Reflection of the Day

Dear Me,

In the journey towards financial empowerment, let the flames of self-trust and growth guide your path. It's time to release the grip of guilt and frustration over past money struggles and embrace the power of forgiveness, allowing the emergence of your ability to save, invest, and make wise financial choices. Remember, you possess the capacity to reshape your financial narrative.

Let go of the weight of past mistakes and regrets. Embrace the power of forgiveness, not for the sake of the money itself, but for your peace of mind and self-worth. By forgiving yourself, you free yourself from financial anxieties and open doors to new financial opportunities.

Understand that everyone faces financial challenges at some point. Release the need to judge yourself harshly for past decisions and instead focus on the lessons learned. Choose to see your financial journey as a pathway to growth and understanding.

Foster a mindset of financial empowerment. Replace self-doubt with self-belief and scarcity thinking with abundance thinking. Embrace the potential for growth and learning in the realm of finances. Trust that you have the skills to make informed decisions.

Recognize that forgiving yourself for money struggles doesn't mean avoiding responsibility. It means letting go of paralyzing guilt and shame to move forward with a clear perspective and renewed determination.

As you move forward, let your heart be a sanctuary of self-trust and financial empowerment. Replace fear of mistakes with confidence in your ability to learn and adapt. Embrace the moments of financial progress and informed choices that have led you to this point.

Nurture your financial wisdom, sowing seeds of mindfulness and empowerment. Choose to see your finances as an area of growth and exploration. By forgiving and embracing your potential, you unleash the power to make informed, confident, and empowering money choices.

With unwavering support and financial empowerment,

[Your Name]

Meditative Thought of the Day

In the sanctuary of self-compassion, I've embraced the journey to forgive my struggles with money. Understanding has woven a tapestry of acceptance, threading connections beyond financial challenges.

With each step towards financial healing, a symphony of empowerment resounds, a celebration of growth and newfound abundance.

The weight of past worries has lifted, replaced by the lightness of financial freedom's promise. In this liberation, I embrace the power to rewrite my relationship with money to create a future shaped by abundance and wisdom. With forgiveness as my guiding principle, I navigate a path of financial empowerment, recognizing that my worth transcends monetary limitations.

The whispers of self-belief eclipse the echoes of scarcity, weaving a tapestry of resilience and prosperity. Amidst the tapestry of financial transformation, I rise, triumphant in the beauty of forgiveness. The journey continues an exploration of financial freedom, a testament to the strength that flourishes when forgiveness paves the way to abundance.

Deeper Connection Within

1. Reflect on the idea of finding gratitude for your struggles. How might reframing them as opportunities for growth and learning help you release guilt and shame?

_____

_____

_____

_____

_____

2. Can you identify positive aspects that have emerged from your journey with forgiveness, negative self-talk, guilt, or shame? How do they contribute to your growth?

_____

_____

_____

_____

_____

3. Reflect on how your past mistakes have shaped your perspective and approach to self-forgiveness. How can you shift these experiences into opportunities for growth?

_____

_____

_____

_____

_____

Loving Statements About Me

Forgiveness is my path to liberation, freeing me from the past's chains.

I choose to forgive not for others but to reclaim my peace and happiness.

Through forgiveness, I find freedom from resentment's heavy burden.

Gratitude Reflection of the Day

I'm grateful for the inner strength that forgiveness fosters, allowing me to face life's challenges with grace.

Inner Reflections

Overcome Your Struggle With A Poverty Mindset

Forgiveness Reflection of the Day

Dear Me,

In the journey of self-transformation, let the light of abundance and growth guide your path. It's time to release the grip of a poverty mindset and open your heart to forgiveness, allowing abundance into your life. Remember, you can shape your relationship with abundance and create a prosperous life.

Let go of the limitations imposed by a poverty mindset. Embrace the power of forgiveness, not because you were wrong, but because you deserve to experience the fullness of life's blessings. By forgiving, you free yourself from the chains of scarcity and open doors to a world of abundance.

Understand that abundance is not just about material possessions; it's about a mindset that recognizes the opportunities and blessings around you. Release the need to dwell on what's lacking and shift your focus to the present moment and its potential.

Foster a mindset of abundance by embracing gratitude. Replace thoughts of scarcity with thoughts of appreciation for what you have. Choose to see the beauty and value in your experiences, relationships, and resources.

Recognize that forgiving your poverty mindset doesn't mean dismissing your struggles. It means choosing to see them as stepping stones towards growth and transformation. By releasing self-imposed limitations, you pave the way for prosperity to flow into your life.

As you move forward, let your heart be a sanctuary of gratitude and abundance. Replace fear of scarcity with a sense of possibility and trust in the flow of life. Embrace the moments of gratitude and contentment that have already enriched your journey.

Nurture your abundance mindset, sowing seeds of positivity and openness. Choose to see life as a canvas where you can paint your dreams and aspirations. By forgiving and embracing the potential for abundance, you unlock the door to a life filled with richness and fulfillment.

With abundant love and support,

[Your Name]

Meditative Thought of the Day

In the sanctuary of self-awareness, I've risen above the struggle to forgive my poverty mindset. Compassion has woven a tapestry of understanding, threading connections beyond limiting beliefs.

With each shift towards abundance, a symphony of transformation resounds, a celebration of growth and renewed perspective. The weight of scarcity thinking has dissolved, replaced by the lightness of abundance's embrace. In this transformation, I embrace the power to rewrite my mindset to manifest a reality rooted in prosperity and positivity.

With forgiveness as my guiding light, I navigate a path of self-empowerment, recognizing that my thoughts shape my reality. The whispers of abundance eclipse the echoes of lack, weaving a tapestry of resilience and expansion. Amidst the tapestry of mindset evolution, I rise, triumphant in the beauty of forgiveness.

The journey continues an exploration of abundance mindset, a testament to the strength that flourishes when forgiveness paves the way to limitless potential.

Deeper Connection Within

1. How might adopting a broader perspective on your journey help you extend compassion and understanding to yourself, ultimately releasing guilt and shame?

_____

_____

_____

_____

_____

2. How can you infuse your daily life with the perspective that your struggles are part of a transformative path toward healing and empowerment?

_____

_____

_____

_____

_____

3. Reflect on your deep desires for self-forgiveness, freedom from guilt, and release from shame. How might you describe these intentions from the depths of your heart?

_____

_____

_____

_____

_____

Loving Statements About Me

As I forgive, I let go of what no longer serves me, making space for growth.

Forgiveness is my bridge to a life free from the weight of unresolved conflicts.

I embrace personal growth as a lifelong journey of self-discovery and improvement.

Gratitude Reflection of the Day

I appreciate the moments when I've extended forgiveness to myself, knowing that self-compassion is a profound act of self-love.

Inner Reflections

Overcome Your Struggle
With Perfectionism

Forgiveness Reflection of the Day

Dear Me,

In the journey towards self-acceptance and growth, let the light of excellence guide your path. It's time to release the grip of perfectionism and open your heart to forgiveness, allowing the transformation from seeking perfection to striving for excellence and doing your best. Remember, you can achieve remarkable outcomes without the weight of unattainable standards.

Let go of the burden of perfectionism that has held you back. Embrace the power of forgiveness, not because you were wrong, but because you deserve to experience the freedom that comes with self-compassion and a pursuit of excellence. By forgiving, you liberate yourself from the chains of unrealistic expectations.

Understand that seeking excellence doesn't mean dismissing high standards. It means recognizing that you are human and growth occurs through learning, evolving, and embracing imperfection. Choose to see the beauty in your progress and the journey of self-improvement.

Foster a mindset of excellence by embracing your uniqueness. Replace the need for flawless outcomes with the understanding that your personal touch brings value to your endeavors. Choose to celebrate the growth journey, acknowledging that making mistakes and learning from them is okay.

Recognize that forgiving yourself for struggles with perfectionism doesn't mean lowering your standards; it means elevating your mental and emotional well-being. Release the grip of self-criticism and create space for self-compassion and self-belief.

As you move forward, let your heart be a sanctuary of self-love and pursuit of excellence. Replace self-doubt with self-assurance and fear of failure with enthusiasm for learning. Embrace the moments of growth, progress, and effort propelling you forward.

Nurture your pursuit of excellence, sowing seeds of self-belief and enthusiasm. Choose to see every endeavor as an opportunity to learn and evolve. By forgiving and embracing your potential for greatness, you open the door to a fulfilling journey where growth and self-love coexist harmoniously.

With unwavering support and the pursuit of excellence,

[Your Name]

Meditative Thought of the Day

In the sanctuary of self-acceptance, I've embraced the journey to forgive my perfectionism. Compassion has woven a tapestry of understanding, threading connections beyond unrealistic standards; with each step towards embracing imperfection, a symphony of authenticity resounds, a celebration of growth and self-discovery.

The weight of relentless expectations has lifted, replaced by the lightness of self-compassion's touch. In this liberation, I embrace the power to rewrite my relationship with achievement to create a future woven with balance and self-love. With forgiveness as my guiding principle, I navigate a path of self-empowerment, recognizing that my worth transcends flawless outcomes—the whispers of self-kindness eclipse the echoes of self-critique, weaving a tapestry of resilience and authenticity.

Amidst the tapestry of personal evolution, I rise, triumphant in the beauty of forgiveness. The journey continues an exploration of self-acceptance, a testament to the strength that flourishes when forgiveness paves the way to embracing my beautifully imperfect self.

Deeper Connection Within

1. How might your understanding of self-forgiveness change as you acknowledge that it's a multifaceted journey rather than a destination?

_____

_____

_____

_____

_____

2. Can you imagine yourself standing on the other side of self-forgiveness, fully embracing your growth and journey? What do you see, feel, and experience?

_____

_____

_____

_____

_____

3. How can you set gentle and transformative intentions, allowing space for progress, setbacks, and self-compassion along the way?

_____

_____

_____

_____

_____

Loving Statements About Me

Every challenge I face is an opportunity for growth, and I approach them with courage.

I am constantly evolving, shedding old layers to reveal my true potential.

My experiences, both triumphs and setbacks, contribute to my continuous growth.

Gratitude Reflection of the Day

I'm thankful for the peace that forgiveness brings to my heart, allowing me to let go of pain and bitterness.

Inner Reflections

Overcome Your Struggle To Forgive Men

Forgiveness Reflection of the Day

Dear Me,

In the journey of understanding and compassion, let the light of open-mindedness and growth guide your path. It's time to release the grip of hurt and resentment towards men and open your heart to forgiveness, allowing the emergence of your ability to see the goodness and kindness in them. Remember, every individual is a complex mixture of experiences and intentions.

Let go of the weight of past disappointments and pain caused by men. Embrace the power of forgiveness, not for their sake, but for your peace and well-being. By forgiving, you free yourself from negativity and make room for healing and understanding.

Understand that kindness and goodness exist within everyone, regardless of gender. Release the need to generalize based on past experiences and instead focus on the potential for positive interactions and growth.

Foster an open-hearted perspective by focusing on individuals rather than stereotypes. Replace assumptions with curiosity and judgments with empathy. Choose to see each person as an individual with their own unique story.

Recognize that forgiving men doesn't mean dismissing past experiences; it means releasing their hold on your emotions. By forgiving, you regain control over your reactions and open the door to healthier relationships and connections.

Let your heart be a sanctuary of openness and understanding as you move forward. Replace mistrust with a willingness to engage and pain with the healing potential. Embrace the moments of connection, shared laughter, and growth that can reshape your perspective.

Nurture your ability to see the goodness in men, sowing seeds of empathy and appreciation. Choose to approach each encounter with an open heart and a desire to understand. By forgiving and embracing the potential for positive interactions, you create a space for meaningful connections to thrive.

With a heart full of empathy and understanding,

[Your Name]

Meditative Thought of the Day

In the sanctuary of healing, I've embraced the journey to forgive men for conscious or subconscious hurt.

Compassion has woven a tapestry of understanding, threading connections beyond pain. With each act of forgiveness, a symphony of unity resounds a celebration of growth and shared humanity. The weight of past wounds has dissolved, making space for the lightness of reconciliation and empathy. In this reconciliation, I can release pain to foster understanding beyond differences.

With forgiveness as my guiding light, I navigate a path of unity, recognizing that every interaction offers an opportunity for healing and connection. The whispers of empathy eclipse the echoes of hurt, weaving a tapestry of resilience and unity. Amidst the tapestry of human connection, I rise, triumphant in the beauty of forgiveness.

The journey continues an exploration of healing and empathy, a testament to the strength that flourishes when understanding bridges the gap.

Deeper Connection Within

1. How might your intentions provide a guiding light and anchor as you navigate the complexities of forgiveness, self-worth, and healing?

_____
_____
_____
_____
_____

2. Reflect on the resources—books, podcasts, workshops, therapy, or supportive relationships—that resonate with your journey. How have they influenced your perspective?

_____
_____
_____
_____
_____

3. How can you prioritize seeking professional guidance, such as therapy or counseling, to navigate the intricate terrain of forgiveness, guilt, and shame?

_____
_____
_____
_____
_____

Loving Statements About Me

Abundance flows effortlessly into my life as I release negativity and embrace positivity.

I attract abundance by fostering a mindset of gratitude, forgiveness, and self-worth.

The universe supports my journey toward empowerment, abundance, and joy.

Gratitude Reflection of the Day

Today, I'm sending kind and forgiving thoughts to all beings, as we are all interconnected on this journey of forgiveness.

Inner Reflections

Overcome Struggle To Forgive Racist People

Forgiveness Reflection of the Day

Dear Me,

In the journey towards inner strength and self-empowerment, let the light of understanding and resilience guide your path. It's time to release the grip of hurt and anger caused by racist individuals and open your heart to forgiveness, allowing the recognition that they don't define your worth or identity. Remember, your value is inherent and cannot be diminished by the ignorance of others.

Let go of the weight of their discriminatory actions and words. Embrace the power of forgiveness, not because they deserve it, but because you deserve the peace that comes from reclaiming your self-worth. By forgiving, you free yourself from their ignorance and create space for healing and self-empowerment.

Understand that their racism is a reflection of their own insecurities and limited perspective. Release the need to internalize their ignorance and instead focus on the strength of knowing your actual value.

Foster a mindset of self-empowerment by focusing on your identity and worth. Replace their hurtful words with affirmations of strength, dignity, and self-love. Choose to see yourself through your accomplishments, potential, and the love surrounding you.

Recognize that forgiving racist individuals doesn't mean dismissing the impact of their actions; it means choosing to rise above their ignorance. By ignoring, you regain control of your emotions and pave the way for personal growth and healing.

As you move forward, let your heart be a sanctuary of self-love and resilience. Replace their hurtful actions with a strong sense of self-identity and self-assurance. Embrace the moments of empowerment, connection, and positive change that have the power to shape your narrative.

Nurture your ability to rise above racism, sowing seeds of self-worth and dignity. Choose to stand tall in ignorance and prejudice, knowing you are defined by your strength and character, not by their hateful words. By forgiving and embracing your worth, you break free from their hold and become a beacon of self-empowerment.

With unwavering self-love and strength,

[Your Name]

Meditative Thought of the Day

In embracing self-liberation, I've shed the weight of resentment and chosen to embrace the radiance of my greatness. The darkness of prejudice no longer defines my path. I am a beacon of strength, walking confidently in my truth, unburdened by the ignorance of others.

With forgiveness as my armor, I rise above the shadows of racism, allowing my spirit to shine brightly. The echoes of hurt transform into the symphony of resilience within me. I recognize my innate worth, untainted by bias, and channel my energy into growth and positive change.

I celebrate the space I've created within, where the negativity of racism cannot linger. Empowered by my greatness, I move forward with purpose and determination. The journey ahead is illuminated by my unwavering light, igniting a path of unity, compassion, and the transformation of a world once marred by prejudice.

Deeper Connection Within

1. Reflect on the individuals who provide unconditional support and understanding as you embark on this transformative journey. How might their presence impact you?

_____

_____

_____

_____

_____

2. How can you intentionally curate a resource network that uplifts and empowers you as you navigate self-forgiveness and healing?

_____

_____

_____

_____

_____

3. How might you strike a balance between seeking external guidance and trusting your internal wisdom as you move forward on your path?

_____

_____

_____

_____

_____

Loving Statements About Me

I empower myself through forgiveness, acceptance, and unwavering self-love.

Through self-empowerment, I radiate positivity and inspire others to do the same.

Empowerment is not given; it is claimed with the conviction of my intentions.

Gratitude Reflection of the Day

I appreciate the courage it takes to forgive and the resilience it builds in my spirit.

Inner Reflections

Overcome Struggle To Forgive People Who Support Racist People

Forgiveness Reflection of the Day

Dear Me,

In the journey towards self-empowerment and resilience, let the light of understanding and authenticity guide your path. It's time to release the grip of frustration caused by those who make excuses for and support racist individuals and open your heart to forgiveness. Embrace the realization that their choices don't define your identity or worth. Remember, you can shape your narrative and choose the path of strength.

Let go of the weight of their misguided opinions and actions. Embrace the power of forgiveness, not because they deserve it, but because you deserve the peace from asserting your self-worth. By forgiving, you free yourself from the chains of their perspectives and create room for healing and self-definition.

Understand that their choices reflect their own biases and limitations. Release the need to seek validation from those who fail to understand your experience and instead focus on your strength and authenticity.

Foster a mindset of self-empowerment by recognizing your agency in defining who you are. Replace the weight of their opinions with affirmations of self-acceptance, self-love, and resilience. Choose to stand firmly in your truth, knowing their inability to see your worth doesn't diminish it.

Recognize that forgiving those who make excuses for racism doesn't mean disregarding their impact; it means choosing to rise above their perspectives. By forgiving, you reclaim your narrative and pave the way for growth and personal empowerment.

As you move forward, let your heart be a sanctuary of self-definition and authenticity. Replace the desire for approval with the strength of honoring your values. Embrace the moments of empowerment, self-expression, and positive change that allow you to shape your story.

Nurture your ability to define yourself, sowing seeds of self-confidence and self-respect. Choose to stand tall in your beliefs and experiences, recognizing that you are the author of your own identity. By forgiving and embracing your power to define yourself, you break free from the limitations of others and step into a future defined by your strength.

With unwavering self-empowerment,

[Your Name]

Meditative Thought of the Day

In the realm of forgiveness and growth, I've transcended the burden of resentment towards those who remain silent in the face of racism. My heart now celebrates a newfound understanding that their choices don't define my journey. Empowered by this realization, I nurture a space of compassion and resilience.

I bask in the joy of self-empowerment, where my voice and actions resonate louder than the silence of complicity. I encourage myself and those I cherish to stand against injustice with unwavering love. Together, we amplify the call for equality and unity, ensuring that our collective voices create ripples of change.

As I embrace this evolved perspective, I celebrate the transformation of hurt into motivation. My path is no longer tangled in resentment but paved with purpose. I radiate the light of awareness and action, fueling a world where everyone stands against racism, united in pursuing a brighter, fairer tomorrow.

Deeper Connection Within

1. Close your eyes and visualize your life after releasing guilt, shame, and negative self-talk. What do you see, feel, and experience in this transformed reality?

_____

_____

_____

_____

_____

2. How does this envisioned future impact your relationships—with yourself, others, and the world around you?

_____

_____

_____

_____

_____

3. Can you identify the feelings, thoughts, and actions you engage with in your future of self-compassion and empowerment?

_____

_____

_____

_____

_____

Loving Statements About Me

I am resilient and strong, capable of rising above the negativity of others and embracing my worth.

I choose to focus on my growth and positive impact, allowing the ignorance of others to fuel my determination.

I advocate for justice and equality, using my voice to challenge racism and create a more inclusive world.

Gratitude Reflection of the Day

I'm grateful for the opportunity to nurture loving energy and kind thoughts within myself, for they are the foundation of forgiveness and inner peace.

Inner Reflections

BONUS

DAY 22

I Forgive People For Lying To Me To "Protect My Feelings"

Forgiveness Reflection of the Day

Dear Me,

In the journey towards inner peace and understanding, let the light of empathy and self-awareness guide your path. It's time to release the grip of hurt caused by those who lied to "protect your feelings" and open your heart to forgiveness. Embrace the realization that their choices were about their fears and vulnerabilities, not a reflection of their worth. Remember, you have the power to free yourself from the burden of their actions.

Let go of the weight of their well-intentioned yet misguided decisions. Embrace the power of forgiveness, not because they deserve it, but because you deserve the peace that comes from knowing the truth and asserting your emotional well-being. By forgiving, you free yourself from the chains of their actions and create space for healing and understanding.

Understand that their lies were born out of their insecurities and worries. Release the need to take

195

their choices personally and focus on your emotional healing and growth.

Foster a mindset of empathy by recognizing that everyone carries their baggage and fears. Replace the need for validation from their words with the understanding that you deserve honesty and respect. Choose to see their lies as a reflection of their struggles, not a commentary on your worth.

Recognize that forgiving those who lied to "protect your feelings" doesn't mean excusing their actions; it means releasing their choices' hold on your emotions. By forgiving, you regain control over your emotional narrative and create a foundation for personal growth and healing.

As you move forward, let your heart be a sanctuary of self-compassion and understanding. Replace the desire for their honesty with the strength of valuing your emotional well-being. Embrace the moments of clarity, growth, and emotional freedom that allow you to release the burden of their lies.

Nurture your ability to navigate emotions, sowing seeds of self-respect and emotional intelligence. Choose to acknowledge your feelings while recognizing that their choices do not reflect your worth. By forgiving and embracing your healing power, you pave the way for a future defined by your emotional strength.

With unwavering self-compassion,

[Your Name]

Meditative Thought of the Day

Having transcended the shackles of deception, I now revel in the liberation of my spirit. The weight of hidden truths and half-truths no longer burdens my heart. Instead, I embrace the power of honesty to myself and others.

With clarity as my guide, I celebrate the authenticity that fills my life. The haze of misleading intentions has lifted, allowing genuine connections and open communication. I find strength in my ability to discern the truth and navigate relationships with transparency.

In this newfound space of honesty, I stand tall and confident in facing the reality of situations. The echoes of past deceptions transform into echoes of resilience within me. I am empowered to uphold my emotional well-being, recognizing that truth is a cornerstone of trust and authentic connection.

As I walk this path, I honor the truth I deserve and offer the same respect to those around me. I celebrate the journey of growth that led me to this point, where my heart is a sanctuary of openness and integrity. With every step, I embrace a life built on genuine interactions, empowered choices, and an unwavering commitment to my worth.

Deeper Connection Within

1. Reflect on the strengths and qualities within you that will play a pivotal role in realizing this future vision. How can you harness them?

_____

_____

_____

_____

_____

2. How might this visualization be a powerful guidepost that influences your choices and helps you stay aligned with your healing journey?

_____

_____

_____

_____

_____

3. How can you approach forgiveness as a pilgrimage of self-discovery, where each step represents a moment of growth and understanding?

_____

_____

_____

_____

_____

Loving Statements About Me

Empowerment is my birthright, and I step into it with every breath.

I am the architect of my destiny, designing a life that aligns with my passions.

Through forgiveness and self-love, I cultivate a life of endless personal expansion.

Gratitude Reflection of the Day

I appreciate the transformative power of forgiveness in my life, as it leads me towards a brighter, more harmonious future.

Inner Reflections

Closing The Chapter Of Unforgiveness

As we draw the final curtain on this transformative journey, the echoes of our footsteps reverberate with the resonance of triumph over adversity. The pages of this book have been our compass, guiding us through the labyrinth of unforgiveness toward the radiant dawn of empowerment. The story we've uncovered, the lessons we've embraced, and the transformations we've witnessed have united us in a tapestry of healing, growth, and newfound strength.

A Tale of Unveiling Truths

Through the pages of this book, we've delved deep into the caverns of unforgiveness—the raw, unfiltered emotions, the haunting echoes of hurt, and the shadows of pain. We've gazed unflinchingly at the scars that marked our souls, recognizing that these scars were not the end of our stories but the beginning of our healing. We've witnessed the power of vulnerability, the strength of confronting our pain head-on, and the liberation that comes when we let go of the burdens we've carried for far too long.

The Birth of Empowerment

In the wake of unforgiveness, we've discovered a wellspring of empowerment. The struggles that once shackled us have become the catalysts for our metamorphosis. Through forgiveness, we've shifted the paradigm from victimhood to agency. We've learned that forgiveness is not a sign of weakness but an assertion of our strength—a proclamation that we refuse to be defined by our wounds.

The empowerment we've cultivated is not a mere fleeting sentiment; it's a profound realization of our capacity to shape our destinies. It's a journey that has shown us the light within us, our resilience, and the uncharted territories we are ready to explore. Our empowerment is the emblem of our courage to dream beyond our limitations, to embrace joy in the face of adversity, and to build a life of abundance from the ruins of the past.

Restoring Connections, Rebuilding Lives

Forgiveness has restored our connections—with others, ourselves, and the world—and provided the cornerstone for rebuilding our lives. The bridges we've crossed between estrangement and reconciliation are testaments to our determination to mend what was broken. We've forged healthier boundaries and rebuilt relationships based on empathy, understanding, and acceptance.

As we move forward, we are architects of a future painted in hues of joy, happiness, and abundance. The wounds of the past are no longer open wounds; they are stories of triumph etched into our beings. With each step, we're constructing a life that resonates with authenticity, kindness, and gratitude.

Seeds of Growth Sown Through Forgiveness

In the fertile soil of forgiveness, we've sown seeds of growth that will yield a bountiful harvest for years to come. The wisdom we've acquired through our struggles has germinated into a newfound perspective that allows us to see challenges as stepping stones and failures as stepping stones toward success. Our journey has taught us that growth is not linear but a mosaic of setbacks and triumphs that weave the fabric of our becoming.

A Heart Filled With Gratitude

As we conclude this chapter, our hearts are grateful for the opportunity to embark on this transformative journey, the lessons that have shaped us, and the community that has walked alongside us. We are grateful for the strength that unforgiveness demanded from us and the resilience that forgiveness cultivated within us.

A Timeless Invitation

The journey we've undertaken does not end with the closing of this book—it's a lifelong odyssey of self-discovery, healing, and growth. It's an invitation to continue cultivating forgiveness, to remain committed to our empowerment, and to live each day with purpose, authenticity, and compassion.

May the stories shared within these pages serve as beacons of hope for those who still tread the path of unforgiveness. May they remind us that healing is possible, that growth is attainable, and that empowerment is within reach. Let us never forget that the power to rewrite our stories, redefine our futures, and build lives imbued with joy, happiness, and abundance rests firmly in our hands.

As we step into the world beyond these pages, let us do so with heads held high, hearts open wide, and an unwavering commitment to forgiving, healing, and growing. Our journey has been a testament to the extraordinary strength of the human spirit, and the legacy we leave behind will forever illuminate the way for others to follow.

With boundless hope and unwavering gratitude,

[Your Name]

Below Is A List Of All 35 Forgiveness Journals

Written By: Tuniscia Okeke

Available on Amazon and other major bookstores or
www.forgivenesslifestyle.com
Instagram: @forgivenesslifestyle
For bulk orders: info@forgivenesslifestyle.com

Forgiving Yourself

Forgiving Your Body Journal

Accepting the Gift of
Forgiveness Journal

Forgiving People Who
Reject You Journal

P.S. Forgive Yourself
First Journal

Who Do You Struggle
To Forgive Journal

Forgiving Your Struggle
With Addiction Journal

Forgiving Your Parents

Forgiving Your Mother Journal

Forgiving Your Father Journal

Forgiving Your Parents Journal

Parenthood

Forgiving and Overcoming
Mom Guilt Journal

Forgiveness Journal for Fathers

Parents Forgiving
Tweens/Teen Journal

Parents Forgiving Adult
Children Journal

Family

Forgiving Dead Loved
One's Journal

Forgiving Family Secrets Journal

Forgiving The Bullies In
Your Family Journal

Forgiving Your Siblings Journal

Marriage

Forgiving Your Wife Journal

Forgiving Your Husband Journal

Forgiving Your Mother-
In-Law Journal

Romantic Relationships

Forgiving Your Ex Journal

Forgiving The "New"
Woman Journal

Teens & Millennials

Forgiveness Journals for Teens

Forgiveness Journal
for Millennials

Religion

Forgiving God Journal

Forgiving Church People Journal

Blended Family

Forgiving A Co-Parent Journal

Forgiveness Journal
for Stepmothers

Forgiving Your
Stepmother Journal

Forgiving Your Stepkids
Mom Journal

Relationships

Forgiving Your Abuser Journal

Forgiving Friends Journal

Business/Finances

Forgiveness In Business Journal

Forgiving People At
Work Journal

Forgiving Past Money
Mistakes Journal

Sending you loving energy as you
forgive, heal, and grow.

www.forgivenesslifestyle.com

Thank You

Gratitude is the thread that weaves connections, and at this moment, I extend my deepest appreciation to those whose unwavering support and love have been the foundation of this 35-journal writing journey and beyond.

To my beloved husband, your unwavering confidence and support during our marriage and this writing project have been my anchor. Thank you for your belief in me. It has been a constant source of inspiration. Your love and presence in my life make my soul smile.

To my mother, your honesty and vulnerability have led to this beautiful healing journey. Your transparency has supported my healing and given me the strength to support others on their transformational journey. I will forever be grateful for your courage to tell the truth.

My dear daughter, Shantia Dajah, your reminder to give myself grace has been a guiding light. Your wisdom transcends your years. You make my heart smile.

To my incredible son, Damien, your encouragement and motivation have fueled my determination to embark on this transformative journey. Your presence in my life is a source of boundless joy.

To Ike, my dynamic youngest son, your cheering from the sidelines has been a source of motivation and warmth. Your enthusiasm lights up my days.

My sister, Tanniedra, your unwavering belief in me and our brainstorming sessions have been invaluable. You are truly a gift.

Little sister, Jazmin, your willingness to share your experiences and vulnerability has touched my heart deeply. Your courage is inspiring.

To my "business bestie," Martha Banks Hall, the Creator of Vision Words, your prayers, encouraging texts, and our deep explorations of thoughts have been a source of clarity and growth to help me birth this project.

Denise, my beautiful friend, "The Fertility Godmother," your enthusiastic voice memos have made me feel like a rock star. Your presence has been a pillar of my strength.

To Thuy, I'm deeply grateful for your accountability and sisterhood, and I hold you as the beautiful gift you are close to my heart.

To Georgette and Cristal, your cheers have lifted my spirits. Your presence in my life is a blessing.

You all hold a special place in my heart, and I thank you from the depths of my soul for being a part of my journey.

Made in the USA
Middletown, DE
15 October 2023

40778972R00126